TOTAL
SHOTMAKING

ALSO BY JOHN ANDRISANI

Learning Golf: The Lyle Way, with Sandy Lyle

Natural Golf, with Seve Ballesteros

101 Supershots, with Chi Chi Rodriguez

The Golf Doctor, with Robin McMillan

Hit It Hard! with Mike Dunaway

Golf Your Way, with Phil Ritson

Grip It and Rip It! with John Daly

TOTAL SHOTMAKING

THE GOLFER'S GUIDE TO LOW SCORING

FRED COUPLES

with JOHN ANDRISANI

CollinsWillow

An Imprint of HarperCollins*Publishers*

All rights reserved

First published in 1994 by
HarperCollins*Publishers*
10 East 53rd Street
New York NY 10022

This edition published in 1994 by
CollinsWillow
an imprint of HarperCollins*Publishers*
London

**A CIP catalogue record for this book
is available from the British Library.**

ISBN 0 00 218522 9

Printed and bound in Great Britain by
Butler & Tanner Ltd, Frome and London

For All My Fans—

For years you have been supporting me at tournaments, and encouraging me in your letters. I hope that this book helps you understand my game better, and helps you play better golf.

CONTENTS

Color photos follow page 112.

FOREWORD

Wherever in the world I travel to teach golf, play it, or watch it, I discover how many fans Fred Couples has.

First and foremost, golfers admire Fred for his shotmaking prowess. But I think another reason Fred is so popular is that the golfing public perceives him to be sincere, and they're right. He's a regular guy, with not one phony streak in him. Truly, with Fred Couples, what you see is what you get.

I first met Fred in 1978, when he was a student at the University of Houston and a member of its golf team. Back then, he and his fellow teammates used to practice at the nearby River Oaks Country Club, where I was, and still am, the head golf professional.

Several years later, during the 1986 PGA Championship, played at the Inverness Country Club, in Toledo, Ohio, Fred casually asked me to analyze his swing, because he was having driving problems. I simply told him to turn his left shoulder behind the ball more. After a few swings, he was back on track, hitting tee shots powerfully and accurately.

In the spring of 1987, Fred and I started to get serious about a teacher-student relationship. Fred telephoned to ask if he could work with me and one of my assistant professionals, Paul Marchand, in Houston for an entire week. As it turned out, he stayed on an extra week—to practice, which is something the media thinks Fred hates to do.

Maybe this misconception stems from the fact that Fred hates to practice if there is no purpose to his practice. In other words, he doesn't practice to kill time. He goes to the practice tee to work on a swing problem, to try to groove a specific move, or to learn a new shot. And make no mistake: he'll spend hours trying to accomplish his goal. A lazy person doesn't do that. A dedicated person does.

Ironically, hard practice is one big reason why Fred has a powerfully rhythmic swing that's reminiscent of Sam Snead's, a superb short game, and an inventive shotmaking game.

I'm glad that he's finally sharing his knowledge on how to play in *Total Shotmaking*. The shots contained in this book will keep Fred winning and will bring your game to such a high level that you're bound to lower your handicap—fast!

Good luck, and have fun.

Dick Harmon

INTRODUCTION

My first memories of Fred Couples were at the University of Houston, when during the late 1970s we were teammates.

We lived across from each other in Taub Hall. Fred was friendly, but on the quiet side.

At the time, Houston had a slew of fine young players; many of them planned to join the PGA Tour soon after graduating. We had more than twenty players on our team; so many that a qualifying round had to be played to determine which six would compete in each tournament.

It was common to sit at dinner with members of the team, discussing the occurrences of the qualifying day. I remember that a disproportionate number of these conversations among some of the country's most talented and fiercely competitive young golfers revolved around some terrific trouble shot or long drive Fred hit. From the beginning, everyone agreed that Fred was something special. How right we were!

Fred possesses great strength, superb flexibility, and extraordinary coordination. These alone are ideal assets for golf. But combine them with a cool temperament and fabulous swing, and it's no surprise why Fred's such a world-class golfer.

In a sport in which overintensity can destroy a player's performance, Fred's casual yet focused approach to the game works best over the long run. Fred doesn't take himself or the game too seriously, and that's one big reason why he will be playing winning golf for a long time to come.

Another reason is that off the course, while taking a lesson from either me or Dick Harmon or both of us together, Fred thinks about his swing and the intricacies of his mechanics. But once on the course, he simply imagines the flight of the ball, swings the club back, then lets "feel" take over.

Because Fred creates exceptionally high clubhead speed during the swing, he is able to curve the ball a large degree and hit it extremely high if needed. Fred also enjoys the challenge of hitting out of trouble or scrambling around the green, which is another reason why he is so good at what he does. In fact, in my mind, there is no better shotmaker than Fred Couples.

Another thing that makes Fred such a fine player is his honesty about his performance. When he's off, he's not too proud to ask for help and work on his shots.

On average, Fred visits Dick and me five times a year. Almost all of our work with Fred centers around a few simple swing fundamentals. There are, however, times when Fred visits us just to practice or play or learn a new shot, either at River Oaks or at Houston Country Club, where I am the golf professional. The reason Fred practices is that he enjoys coming as close as possible to perfecting a game that was never meant to be perfected.

Fred is determined on the course, too, even though during a tournament he sometimes looks like he's strolling in the park. Take it from me, Fred's not daydreaming. He's merely in his "office," concentrating on the work at hand and performing to the best of his ability. On days when he does, no one in the world can match him.

Like his parents and family, I'm proud of this humble superstar. I'm proud of a kid who grew up with a deep love for golf and despite fame and fortune never got too big for his britches. Last, I'm happy that Fred Couples has written *Total Shotmaking*, for it truly is a guidebook to lower scores.

Paul Marchand

TOTAL
SHOTMAKING

1 | MY GAME AND YOURS

A Carefree Mind-set and a Creative Practice Program
Are Critical to Becoming a Shotmaking Virtuoso

Many enthusiasts who have watched me play professional golf probably think I'm a "natural" who was blessed at birth with the God-given talent to boom three-hundred-yard drives straight down the middle of the fairway, loft medium and long irons high and dead on line with the flagstick, recover with Houdini-like skill from terrible lies in rough, and save par from around the green by hitting superhuman, soft-landing finesse shots.

I will admit that inheriting the same strong, *quick* hands that made my father a star semipro baseball home-run hitter has helped me hit powerful tee shots. I suppose, too, that being blessed with my dad's tremendous hand-eye coordination has made me a more gifted iron and short-game player. But the main reasons I'm the golfer I am today have to do with much more than just my genes.

One reason for my success as a professional is that for the most part I taught myself to swing a golf club, which explains why my loose-looking, long-swing technique is somewhat unorthodox but so *natural feeling* that it's very easy to repeat consistently, even when the pressure is on during a championship. Make no mistake, grooving a swing that repeats itself should be your *top* priority.

I also practiced hitting out of a variety of lies, to see which club and what recovery method worked best. Sometimes, too, I would hit short green-side shots with low-lofted irons just to see how the ball would react in the air and on the ground. This trial-and-error process helped me—and will help you, too—evolve into a more versatile shotmaker. Let me prove that to you.

Drop a few balls in fluffy lies in the fringe grass bordering your local practice chipping green. Next, with a three-iron that features a mere twenty-four degrees of loft, try to hit short chips to a pin about twenty feet away. After hitting just a few low-flying "hot" shots over the green, you'll realize that to loft the ball softly into the air and onto the green, so that it trickles to the hole, you will have to play the ball forward in your stance with your hands slightly behind it, lay the clubface wide open, keep more weight on your right foot, swing the club back on an upright plane, and finally, drop the club gently down so that its sole contacts a spot in the grass about an inch behind the ball.

By practicing creatively with a three-iron you will force yourself to invent a new recovery technique—a new shot. The added bonus: the same shotmaking principles can be used to recover from a variety of course situations. The only difference is that you would change clubs, lengthen your swing, and quicken your tempo slightly. So, in a sense, you teach yourself not one but many new recovery shots.

The other important reason for my success is my reserved mindset. I have never taken the game too seriously. From the time I started to play golf, I promised myself that I would play the sport only for fun. Even now that is why I play, and I have my *carefree* attitude to thank for that.

The press still considers me one of the most laid-back athletes since Babe Ruth. That's supposed to be a criticism, but I consider it a compliment because I think being carefree on the course is one of the secrets to scoring well consistently. I'm not saying you should whistle "Summertime" while you're hitting shots. But I do think that when you're carefree, you're relaxed; and when you're relaxed, you swing more freely. All of which means you are going to generate maximum clubhead speed on drives. On irons, you'll be less apt to steer the shot, which is one of the most common faults among club-level players.

I think many amateurs who mistakenly treat golf as a life-or-death situation try to stay as seriously focused during a leisurely round of golf as Ben Hogan (the "Wee Iceman") was during his heyday. Hogan was a sensational player of a special breed, who played a "different" game. Average golfers, however, who emulate Hogan's style of playing in a cocoon of intense concentration, from the first tee to the final green, usually tighten up on the course. Consequently, their swing doesn't flow and, the shots don't find the fairway or the flagstick. What's worse, these golfers become so worried about protecting their score that when they slip up on just one hole they become mentally undone for the rest of the round—and day!

Whenever discussion at the nineteenth hole turns to players with the best on-course attitude or mind-set, I cite Lee Trevino and Fuzzy Zoeller as models. These two pros joke with the gallery between shots, but once over the ball they truly get down to business, giving each shot such full attention that their concentration level is 100 percent. What's more, if they hit a shot that fails to fly in the planned direction, they don't become upset. They remain calm, never losing sight of one very important truism: *Golf is only a game.* It will, by its very nature, drive you crazy if you let it. I simply don't let it.

I can attribute my superrelaxed frame of mind and carefree on-

Most amateurs will perform better on the course if they adopt the carefree attitude of Lee Trevino *(left)*, rather than the very serious mind-set of Ben Hogan *(right)*.

course attitude to the way I was introduced to golf. Unlike so many of my contemporaries, I didn't have a personal instructor to teach me the fundamentals of a golf swing. I didn't own a brand-new set of custom-made golf clubs. I didn't belong to a classy country club. I wasn't being groomed to become a pro. I played several sports, such as soccer, but not golf—until one day, when I was eleven years old, my brother's best friend and teammate on the Seattle University baseball team gave me a set of used golf clubs. I hit a few shots, and I was hooked.

Jefferson Park, in Seattle, was our local nine-hole public course. Even back then, in 1970, when course design and maintenance standards weren't nearly as high as they are today, the Park wasn't anything special. The average hole was 135 yards, and there was only one par four, measuring 260 yards. Still, whenever I got the chance, I would ride my bicycle to Jefferson and pay a couple of bucks to hack the ball around for a few hours. By the time I turned thirteen, I could pretty much predict in what direction I was going to hit the ball. So I started playing with older, more experienced golfers who could teach me more about the rules, etiquette, and shotmaking and give me a taste of tough competition, too.

During the summertime, a bunch of these guys and I would play "skins" games from early morning to dark. Playing golf with this group and doing some light wagering were also good initiations into what it was like to compete under pressure.

What encouraged me to let out the shaft, however, were the games I had played with my close friend Jay Turner and his dad. Wherever the back tee markers were situated, Jay's dad would have us tee up a couple of yards farther behind them. That way, we really had to hit drives long and straight to have a chance to score par. To keep in training, Jay and I would hit buckets of balls at Jefferson Park's driving range, where we both worked.

I played golf in Catholic high school, too, with teammates who weren't really true golfers. But we always had fun, particularly on away match days, when we were permitted to leave school early in the morning. Our coach packed us in a van, and then we'd all ferry across Puget Sound to play a match at Bainbridge Island or Port Angeles. I would usually return home fairly late at night, exhausted but still excited; and win or lose, I'd lay my head on my pillow with fond memories of the day's adventure.

My college days at the University of Houston were fun, too. Competing on the school golf team further helped me evolve as a player. In 1978, I was named All-American. That same year, I won the Washington State Amateur and Open titles. The highlight of 1978, however, was finishing low amateur in the U.S. Open Golf Championship, which was played at Denver's famous Cherry Hills course. Still, even in light of those successes at golf, I was not thinking seriously about turning professional. The way it happened was kind of crazy.

While staying in Long Beach, California, with a friend, I went to a nearby course and asked the pro if I could play in the Queen Mary Open, which the club was hosting. He said, "Sure, if you turn pro and pay the two-hundred-and-fifty-dollar entry fee."

The next day, when the tournament started, the uncle of Tom Lamore, a college friend of mine, paid my way. He also wired five hundred dollars to the PGA Tour Q-School; that's where wannabes try to qualify to play the PGA Tour full time.

I finished sixth in the Queen Mary and won around three thousand dollars. I also picked up an extra few hundred bucks in the Pro-Am. I was so excited that, after repaying Tom's uncle, I called my father to tell him the good news. He listened intently until I said that I was going to put college on hold while I pursued a pro-golf career. When he heard that, he slammed the phone down.

My father, who was a Seattle Parks employee, knew how hard it was to make a good living from professional golf. So he didn't want me to throw away a college scholarship and the chance to get a good education and "be somebody." Neither did my mother. From my point of view, I was having fun and that was all that mattered. I guess if I would have thought seriously about the real-life consequences and the odds against me, I would have stayed in school and studied harder than ever.

But, what did I know? I was just a young kid who loved golf and took everything in stride. This is where my carefree attitude about life and the game helped me survive—and succeed. I just teed it up and played the game, shot by shot, hole by hole, similar to the way I played life, one day at a time. This is probably why I qualified for the Tour on my first attempt, whereas others my age went back several times or gave up after failing.

My inaugural year on the Tour was 1981. That season, I earned a little more than seventy-five thousand dollars, which was more than any other rookie. Ironically, it was more than I would have made my first year out of college, had I graduated from a top law school and joined a prestigious firm.

In 1982, I finished fifty-third on the money list for the second year in a row.

In 1983, I won my first tournament, the Kemper Open. That one victory helped boost my yearly earnings to more than two hundred thousand dollars; good enough for nineteenth place on the money list. Still, I was basically just another face on the Tour until 1984, when as an underdog I held off Seve Ballesteros, Tom Watson, and Lee Trevino to win the Tournament Players Championship, which many consider to be golf's "Fifth Major." From that moment my life changed, owing to the sudden attention from the golf press and the galleries.

Back then, when off the course, I was sort of a Howard Hughes type. I preferred staying home—and fooling around with my classic cars (such as my 1968 Shelby Mustang) or watching reruns of old *Andy Griffith* and *Leave It to Beaver* shows—to going out. The reason I stayed home was that I couldn't handle all the attention I was suddenly getting. Don't misunderstand me, I realized how important the fans were. And there was nothing I enjoyed more than giving a kid an autograph. All the same, I considered the golf course my office, and when I was away from it, I needed my privacy. I had nothing against shaking hands with a group of golf fans who happened to be sitting at a nearby table in a restaurant. The problem was that so many people would approach me during dinner that my food would become cold before I had a chance to eat it. (Today, because of the endorsement contracts I have with such companies as Lynx, Ashworth, and Cadillac, I come in close contact with corporate executives as well as the general public when I play in a Pro-Am or attend a sponsorship day. So now I'm better at dealing with crowds. Maybe I'm not as good as Arnold Palmer in the public relations category, but, then, who is? I'm still taking lessons from the "King" in that department.)

In 1985 and 1986, I failed to win a single tournament. In 1987, I got off to a slow start again, so in the spring of that year, I did something I had never done before in my entire life: I took a one-week golf lesson from teacher Dick Harmon and one of my college buddies, Paul Marchand, who worked for Dick at the River Oaks Country Club in Houston, Texas.

My classic car collection provides a healthy escape from the pressures of the PGA Tour.

To my surprise, Dick and Paul didn't tell me I had to change my strong grip, my unusual outside-the-target-line take-away, or my unique right-elbow-out position at the top of the swing. Thankfully, they were not method teachers. Therefore, they didn't care about some of my idiosyncrasies, as long as I looked like every other pro when I arrived at the one swing position that matters most: impact. My "professional" friends gave me some simple things to work on and told me why my swing worked, so in case it broke down on the course, I would know how to fix it, much the same way that knowing about the guts of a car engine allows a top mechanic to repair it on the road.

My week-long Houston lesson helped me repeat a good swing more consistently and confidently. Which is one big reason why I won the 1987 Byron Nelson Classic and finished the season winning almost four hundred and ninety thousand dollars.

The following year I earned even more money. And 1989 was an even better year, though a poor performance in the Ryder Cup (a biennial match between a team of twelve pros from the United

States and a team of twelve pros from the UK and Europe) ruined it.

On the last day of the matches, I missed an easy putt on hole seventeen to take the lead in a critical match against Irishman Christy O'Connor. Then, on the eighteenth, I missed the green with a nine-iron; that one bad shot cost me the match and America the Ryder Cup. Had I even tied the match, the U.S. team would have won the coveted cup. Had it not been for the support of veterans Tom Watson and Ray Floyd (after my loss, they assured me that I would learn from my experience and become a better player), I don't know if I ever could have bounced back from this all-time low point in my career. At that juncture, golf had stopped being fun.

Floyd and Watson were right; that defeat made me even more determined to practice harder and play better. I finished ninth on the money list in 1990 and was happy with my standard of golf, except during the PGA Championship, when some bad putting down the stretch cost me the title.

In 1991, victories in the Federal Express St. Jude Classic and the B.C. Open helped me finish third on the money list. The most satisfying part of my year, however, was redeeming myself in the Ryder Cup, which the United States won after a fierce battle at the Kiawah Island Resort's Ocean Course, in South Carolina. As partners in the foursomes match, Ray Floyd and I defeated Bernhard Langer and Mark James. Ray and I also defeated Nick Faldo and Ian Woosnam. With Payne Stewart, I earned a half point by tying Seve Ballesteros and José Maria Olazabal. In the singles, I beat veteran Sam Torrance.

In the winter of 1991, I beat a star-studded field in the Johnnie Walker World Championship, held at the Tryall Golf Club in Jamaica. Although this was not a PGA Tour event, outplaying the best golfers in the game boosted my confidence to a new level and readied me for 1992. What it didn't ready me for was a rude awakening from the press.

The press didn't care much about my money winnings, or that I had redeemed myself in the Ryder Cup, or that I had won the World

Championship. If I were to be considered a legitimate superstar, I would have to win one of golf's four major championships: the Masters, the British Open, the U.S. Open, or the PGA. Deep down I knew that they were right. I was still Mr. Cool on the course, but I suddenly had a burning desire to win one of those coveted events. The 1992 Masters was the first one in my sights. Playing at the Augusta National Golf Club, which I just love, my game really clicking along, I was confident something good would happen there.

Heading into the Masters, I was 186 under par for my last eighteen American starts. I had fifteen top-six finishes in those tournaments, and had amassed over $1.7 million in winnings during that stretch. Included in this streak was a win in a playoff against my good friend Davis Love in the Los Angeles Open at the fabulous Riviera Country Club. Also, I won the Nestlé Invitational, held at Arnold Palmer's Bay Hill Club and Lodge in Orlando, Florida. My last competitive appearance before the Masters was a thirteenth-place finish at the Players' Championship, featuring a course-record 63 in round three.

The week prior to the Masters, I reported to Harmon and Marchand again. They had me stand less open to the target line, so that an imaginary line running across my toes ran practically parallel to the ball-target line. I hit some nice high draw shots that work so nicely on the dogleg left holes at Augusta National. (Before, my feet pointed so far left of the target that I tended to swing the club too much on an in-to-out swing path and on too upright a plane. When I did that and my timing wasn't quite in sync, I'd hit the occasional block-slice, which, for a pro like me, is very costly.)

My work with those two top-notch Texas-based golf instructors seemed to be paying off, as was Watson's tip to concentrate harder on the final nine holes and Floyd's advice to try to make any lead I held in a tournament even bigger. Knowing full well how great I was playing, I must confess to getting ahead of myself before the Masters. I just couldn't stop thinking about Augusta.

I pictured myself driving up Magnolia Drive, the famous tree-lined entranceway to the Augusta National Golf Club, the venue

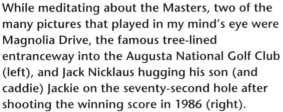

While meditating about the Masters, two of the many pictures that played in my mind's eye were Magnolia Drive, the famous tree-lined entranceway into the Augusta National Golf Club (left), and Jack Nicklaus hugging his son (and caddie) Jackie on the seventy-second hole after shooting the winning score in 1986 (right).

each year for the prestigious Masters. I thought of the trophy case in the clubhouse, displaying golf clubs that past winners had contributed. I thought of the annual dinner, for past champions only, such as Gene Sarazen, Sam Snead, Tom Watson, Arnold Palmer, Gary Player, Gay Brewer, and Jack Nicklaus. I thought of tradition and, a split-second later, of the fabulous amateur player Bobby Jones and the fantastic architect Scotsman Alister Mackenzie who together built the challenging and magnificent Augusta National course. I thought of Sarazen's famous double eagle on the par-five fifteenth hole, where he hit a four-wood shot 235 yards into the cup. I thought of Ben Hogan and the games of perfection he played at Augusta. I thought of Ken Venturi who, as a young man, almost made history by winning the Championship as an amateur. I thought of the big, beautiful, undulating, perfectly manicured greens that can be so punishing. I thought of what one man once said: "Playing golf at Augusta is such a peaceful experience that you get the feeling you are in a cathedral." I thought of all the colorful flowers set out behind the greens, where a nursery once was. I thought of Jack Nicklaus winning the Masters at age forty-six and hugging his son Jackie, who caddied for him. I thought of the wild cheers of the gallery echoing off the tall pine trees that line the fairways of the awesomely picturesque Augusta National golf course. I thought of how ironic it would be if Jim Nantz, my former suitemate at the University of Houston who covers the Masters for CBS television, were to interview me during the postvictory green jacket ceremony in Augusta's Butler Cabin. (Once while watching the Masters on television when we were in college, Jim turned to me, as the winner walked off the final green, and said, "Fred, one day that's going to be you.") I thought of Frederick Stephen Couples making history.

Whenever the subject of the 1992 Masters comes up at a press conference or among fans, nine out of ten people usually want to hear about what happened to me on Sunday, the final day of the championship, on Augusta National's twelfth hole.

The twelfth is a par-three hole, measuring a mere 155 yards. Its name is "Golden Bell," and from the tee it's truly a thing of beauty, especially in spring, during Masters Week, when the azaleas behind Augusta's greens are in full bloom. But don't be fooled; beneath that hole's innocent green beauty lurks a fierce beast. Trust me, the twelfth at Augusta is anything but an ordinary one-shot hole.

The green is so very narrow that there really is no fat area on it to hit to and bail out. Therefore, no matter where the flag is situated—center, front, back, left, right, your eyes are drawn to it. For some inexplicable reason your mind directs your body to aim at it, so you swing to attack the hole. Strategically, this is a big mistake, particularly on Sunday when the pin is always placed on the far right corner of the green.

The player who hits a tee shot short of the Sunday "sucker pin"

A side view of "Golden Bell," Augusta National's pretty, but often punishing, twelfth hole.

must worry about the ball landing in a deep bunker or finishing in Rae's Creek. Between those two treacherous hazards that guard the front of the green, there is a manicured steep bank that has historically drawn the ball back into the creek. If the ball rolls into the drink (or flies into it), the player incurs a one-shot penalty stroke and must drop and replay another ball, which usually means he will end up scoring bogey—or worse!

For the player who attacks the Sunday sucker pin and hits the shot long and left, another big bunker awaits. Landing in it means he must hit a downhill sand shot to a superquick green that slopes away from the player, while staring at Rae's Creek, which lurks only a few yards behind the hole.

The player who misses all of the hazards and the green must face a delicate chip off very tightly mowed grass, which is no bargain either, because with no cushion underneath the ball it's hard to put any loft on the shot and stop it near the hole.

All of these visions, plus the fact that throughout history the balls of players such as Tom Weiskopf have met with a watery grave here, ran through my head as I stood on the tee on Sunday, with an eight-iron in my hand and a two-shot lead over former Masters winner Ray Floyd.

I knew that to avoid disaster, I had to keep the ball left of the hole and on the green. But for some reason, I couldn't prevent my body from steering my swing and the shot toward the flag. When I watched my fade shot fall short of the green and hit the bank, I figured I had thrown my lead away for sure. That's because it's a "given" that a ball hitting the bank short of the green rolls into the water. My ball rolled backward, then trickled, and trickled, and trickled—then stopped! Miraculously, my ball had come to rest short of Rae's Creek. I was alive and could still win the one championship I had dreamed about winning since the day I decided to turn pro.

All I could think of when facing the short, but difficult, mini-pitch shot off an uphill lie on the bank was, "Fred, take advantage of the luckiest break of your life." I did. If I say so myself, I hit the most exacting little shot of my life, landing the ball a foot from the hole, in tap-in range.

It's part of history that I went on to win the green jacket that year—and I know some say that luck got me there. Well, when I analyze my overall performance over four days and seventy-two holes, I admit that luck played a role on Sunday. Good and bad bounces are part of the game. However, luck didn't get me to the winner's circle. I shot rounds of 69, 67, 69, and 70. To shoot those scores at Augusta, you need more than a rabbit's foot or a four-leaf clover in your pocket. You need to possess a skillful *total-shotmaking* game. On those four days in April 1992, I'm proud to say that I brought that kind of game to Augusta and took home the green jacket.

I rounded out the 1992 season by winning the World Cup with Davis Love, my partner, and finished the year in the number one position on the PGA Tour's money list, with earnings of $1,344,188. I was honored to be voted Player of the Year (for the second year in

Being presented with the prestigious green jacket, by defending Masters Champion Ian Woosnam, was the highlight of my 1992 golf season and a moment I shall cherish forever.

a row) by my peers on the Tour. Last but not least, for the second straight year I won the prestigious Vardon Trophy for having the lowest stroke average.

Considering that I had experienced some personal difficulties in 1993, I was pretty happy about playing well enough to win the Honda Classic and Kapalua International tournaments.

In team competition, I'm most proud of my repeat victory in the World Cup, with partner Davis Love, and also the Dunhill Cup victory I earned with teammates John Daly and Payne Stewart.

What was most satisfying about playing so well in the Cups was knowing that most of the shots I hit to win I learned long ago as a kid while practicing with that used set of clubs given to me by my brother's friend.

Developing a full repertoire of shots is an art worth learning, because the more shots you have in your bag, the better you'll score.

In the upcoming chapters, I'll talk about more magical shots I've hit during tournaments. I'll give you a series of playing lessons, starting from the tee and working you down the fairway to the putting green. So you'll learn how to hit these same shots and new shots, too.

Your first lesson will teach you the benefits of cloning my natural-feeling unorthodox grip, plus my pro-style stance and posture. Once you learn how to assume a comfortable, correct setup, I'll teach you how to swing the long clubs, and in my "clinics," I'll give you sophisticated instructions such as how to select the perfect driver and how to add distance to your drives.

My lessons on the short swing will include instruction on how to impart backspin on the ball and how to hit both the soft pitch and pitch-and-run shots.

In *Total Shotmaking*, you'll also learn new ways to hit chips and sand shots, putt cross-handed, and escape from trouble.

In this book, I take shotmaking to a totally different dimension, teaching you everything I ever learned from practicing alone as a kid and playing against the greatest professionals in the world. However, I must confess one thing: *I'm still learning.* In fact, just the other day a friend told me of a new shot he had learned from watching golf on CBS. During the "stroke-savers" segment, Ken Venturi showed how, by taking a four-iron and digging down into the sand with it at impact, you can blast the ball out of a buried lie in a green-side bunker—better than with a wedge!

Total Shotmaking is your guidebook to dealing with practically every possible situation you will probably ever confront on the course. However, teaching yourself new techniques, as I did the cross-handed putting style, can be fun, too. The best way to do this is through trial-and-error practice. Here's how it works.

During practice, change your stance from square to open to closed, alter your grip pressure from light to firm, change your swing plane from upright to flat, set the clubface closed or open, instead of square. Try different combinations of these technical elements (for example, open stance, light grip pressure, open clubface position, and flat swing path) when hitting short and long shots with a variety of clubs.

This probably sounds like a tedious process. But if you let your imagination run wild, practice will be fun and you might even learn a new shot. If you do, record it in a notebook and register it in your brain. *One more thing:* send the instructions along to Fred Couples, care of the PGA Tour.

2 | THE LONG SWING

From Start to Finish

The main objective of the swing with the driver, fairway metals, and longer irons is to deliver the clubhead squarely into the back of the ball, propelling it toward the target with maximum speed and energy. Therefore, from start to finish, the emphasis should be on *freedom of movement*.

Generally, the swings of high-handicap players don't look like "swings" at all. Instead, they look like a series of individual mechanical movements, which the golfer has perhaps worked on quite carefully and diligently. But these individual swing "pieces" seem disconnected—they're firing with no synchronization, like a badly tuned car engine. There are some good positions in the swings of such players, but there's no freedom or flow to their actions.

Employing a high-quality golf swing involves more than just setting the club in the right positions at address, during the take-away, at the top of the swing, while starting down, through the impact zone, and into follow-through. A pro-style technique involves a natural, free-flowing, balanced, speed-producing swinging action of the clubhead. I believe that if you can develop the long swing with this holistic approach in mind, most of those individual key positions that you see illustrated in golf magazines will fall into place without your making them happen.

As good as Jack Nicklaus swings, you shouldn't copy his technique, or any other pro's, exactly to the letter.

I also believe that within the framework of balance, tempo, and good timing, there's room for individuality in the golf swing. Golfers shouldn't try to force themselves to swing exactly like Ben Hogan or Jack Nicklaus or, for that matter, like Fred Couples. Golfers come in all sizes, shapes, degrees of flexibility, degrees of coordination, and degrees of strength. To try to make all golfers follow a single swing recipe would be doing them a great disservice.

The goal is not to make your swing a clone of mine. However, within the limits of your individual physical makeup, I do encourage you to develop a simple, natural, balanced, long, *free* swing through the ball. With these thoughts in mind, let's discuss the factors in the grip and setup that will contribute to this flowing, balanced swing.

THE GRIP: A COMFORTABLE HOLD IS OKAY

Thousands, maybe millions, of words have been written about how to hold the golf club. Frankly, I think a lot of this analysis is overdone. Your golf grip should do two things and two things only:

1. Provide a stable hold on the club through the entire motion, yet allow the free hinging of the wrists and arms.
2. Be comfortable.

Yes, your grip should feel *comfortable.* I've read books that have suggested that if your grip feels comfortable, something's wrong with it. I don't think that makes much sense. If your grip isn't comfortable, you'll be aware of it before and during the swing, and that insecurity will undermine your confidence. The natural, comfortable position of your hands at address is the position you're most likely to return to through impact. If you start with a comfortable hold and with the clubface square to the target line, you're likely to return your hands (and the clubface) the same way.

I use an *overlap*-style grip in which (for the right-handed player) all fingers of the left hand are placed on the grip. My left hand is turned a shade clockwise on the handle so that my left thumb is positioned just to the right of the top center of the handle. Thus the back of my left hand does not point directly at the target but faces somewhat upward as well. My checkpoint is that as I look

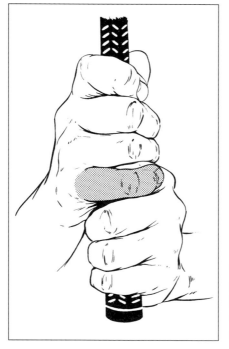

The overlap grip is my choice and that of most pros on the PGA Tour because it keeps the hands securely wedded together throughout the swing.

down, I can see the top knuckles of only my index and middle fingers. (*Note:* I don't wear a glove on my left hand, because I think it detracts from the best possible feel I can obtain.)

I place my right hand on the club so that its palm is square or flush with my left palm. That is, the palm of my right hand faces a shade upward, instead of directly at the target. The three middle fingers of my right hand close around the grip, while my right little finger overlaps the index finger of my left hand. My right palm then closes over my left thumb. The finished right-hand position sees the right thumb resting on the top left portion of the grip itself.

This overlapping position helps wed the two hands securely together throughout the swing. Also, the closer the hands are together on the grip, the more speed you'll generate in the swing.

At this point, I'd like to mention a slightly modified hold that's perfectly acceptable: the *interlocking* grip. Everything in this grip is the same as the overlap grip, except that instead of the right little finger overlapping the left index finger it interlocks or intertwines with it. Some golfers, particularly those with small hands, feel this interlocking position offers a bit more security. If this adjustment suits you, I certainly encourage you to use it, as long as the overall positioning of both hands is as described above.

In my finished grip, both hands are turned a bit more to the right on the club than some other players may prefer. This is known as a relatively "strong" grip position. This kind of hold, it is often said, encourages the hands to turn over excessively through the impact zone so that the clubface contacts the ball in a closed position, pointing left of the target. Thus, it's argued, a strong grip position leads to hooked shots that fly well left of target.

By contrast, a "weak" position is one in which the palms are turned more to the left on the handle, so that the left thumb rests exactly on top of the shaft. From this position, the typical club-level player's hands release is hindered, causing the clubface to be open at impact and the ball to be pushed or sliced to the right.

Which grip position would I say is right for you? I strongly recommend that you forget this strong/weak terminology and, given that your other fundamentals are sound, let the flight of the ball be your guide. If you're hooking (while following the setup and alignment guidelines we'll get into shortly), consider turning both hands a touch counterclockwise on the grip. If you're consistently slicing, you'd do just the opposite—turn your hands a bit more clockwise on the handle to encourage squaring the face at impact.

Many experts have criticized my grip as being too strong. My answer is that this is the hand position from which I consistently return the clubface squarely to the ball. So it's obviously the right position for me. Owing to my "cuppy" strong grip position, I gain a lot of speed by actively whipping my arms and wrists through the impact area. Ironically, I think my left-hand position keeps me

Paul Azinger, the 1993 PGA Champion, is a professional who has had great success using a strong grip.

from closing the clubface excessively through impact. I might add that a couple of current stars, Bernhard Langer and Paul Azinger, use an even stronger grip than I do. So don't be afraid to experiment with the so-called strong position.

One often-overlooked factor regarding the grip is the amount of pressure you exert on the club. I believe in almost all situations you should hold the club very lightly. This is a really significant factor in the grip. A light grip allows you to release your hands and wrists naturally through the impact zone. Meanwhile, a tight grip will restrict your hand and forearm muscles, which often leads to an open clubface and so reduces vital clubhead speed. The result: a weak slice shot.

My grip is so light that I sometimes let go of the club with my right hand after impact. This might seem extraordinary, but it definitely shows that my grip pressure was light through impact, which is one key reason why I consistently drive the ball a long distance. By contrast, I think most amateurs strangle the club and thus get in their own way, as far as creating strong clubhead speed is concerned. Their arms and wrists are locked and their tight upper bodies hit at the ball too much.

There's a device on the market that measures the golfer's grip pressure at address and throughout the swing. You might be interested to know that the pressure in most Tour pros' grips at address is only about 10 percent of the average club player's maximum. So trust yourself to take a nice, light hold on the club as you set up to the ball. If anything, I'd recommend you grip the club a tad more firmly in your left hand than your right (for a righty player). A nice soft right-hand hold means a freer release through impact. Avoid tension in the arms at all costs.

STANCE AND SETUP POSITION—GET COMFORTABLE

Now let's get you in position to make a smooth flowing swing. With the driver, you should assume a relatively wide stance for added stability—the distance between your heels should be about as wide as your shoulders. As the clubs get shorter, your stance will gradually narrow.

In assuming my address, I turn both of my feet out about twenty-five degrees. This stance helps my body turn on both the backswing and the downswing. Some pros advocate keeping your right foot perpendicular to the target line; this foot position acts as a "governor" on your backswing turn. In my opinion, on drives in particular, you can't have enough backswing turn as long as you retain your balance. So turn the toes out a bit.

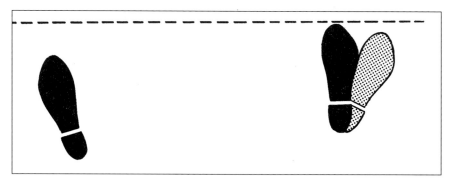

Pointing both of my feet out, practically Charlie Chaplin style, promotes a full and free turning action of my body during the swing.

As you assume your address posture, flex your knees just slightly. Don't bend your knees deeply, as many amateurs who top the ball do. When you overflex you rise slightly through the impact zone; just a little upward movement is enough to cause a mis-hit shot.

In the correct setup position, you'll bend slightly more from the waist, with your back about fifteen to twenty degrees from vertical. You should feel you're in a very relaxed position with your arms hanging straight down, about six inches away from your body. I am very aware of establishing an angle of my spine bent forward at the waist. This serves as the axis of my very aggressive rotation both on the backswing and through-swing.

For the driver, I set up with my hands a tad behind the ball; this allows me to use the full loft of the clubhead at impact. It also helps me feel like I will start my arms and shoulders together. If you position your hands ahead of the clubface at address, you'll shut the clubface too much, which hinders your ability to launch the drive on the proper trajectory. I believe it also encourages too much arms action as you start the swing. Because most amateurs have trouble hitting the ball as high as they'd like, this small adjustment may help you too.

In the driver swing, you want to swing the clubhead through the ball with a sweeping action—not with a sharp downward blow. To help you achieve this, play the ball forward in your stance with your head behind it.

You may have noticed from watching me play in tournaments that for all shots, even the drive, my stance alignment is somewhat open, or points to the left of a direct line from my ball to the target. I've found over the years that this open alignment works best for me—even better than a perfectly square position in which lines across the feet, knees, hips, and shoulders all run parallel to the target line. The rea-

Setting up with your hands behind the ball will encourage a powerful upswing hit.

son for this is that I have such a big shoulder turn going back, and my downswing drops the clubhead inside the line it took on the backswing. Consequently, although my alignment is a little open, I deliver the clubhead straight down the target line and then quickly around my body to the left. In this regard, my swing action is a little like Lee Trevino's.

However, just because I swing effectively from an open body alignment, doesn't mean everyone else will. Most amateurs should strive to align as squarely to the target line as possible. That is, lines drawn across your toes, knees, hips, and shoulders should all be more or less parallel to an imaginary line that runs from the ball to the target.

Have a friend check your alignment periodically on the practice

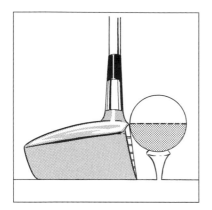 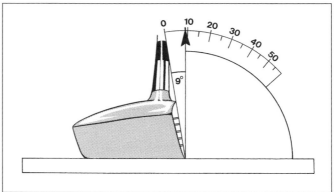

On drives, tee the ball up fairly high (left), particularly if your driver features nine degrees of loft (right).

tee. Then observe whether this square position lets your personal swinging action deliver the club straight down the target line and then around to the left. If you're hitting a straight ball consistently at the target, great. If you consistently pull the ball a little left, a slightly closed stance—as used by greats Arnold Palmer and Gary Player—may suit you. If you consistently tend to push your shots a bit right, you'll know that opening your alignment a touch could do the trick for you. Controlled experimentation is highly worthwhile. This allows you to make small adjustments on the course when necessary.

One last point regarding the driver setup: I recommend that you tee the ball up fairly high—at least half the ball should be above the top of the driver's clubface. This will encourage you to sweep the ball away just as the clubhead begins to ascend from its lowest point, particularly if, like me, you swing a driver that features nine degrees of loft.

TAKE-AWAY AND BACKSWING: A LIGHT AND LIMBER SET-AND-ROTATE MOVE

Now, we're set to draw the club back from the ball. I'm going to suggest a couple of points that might seem slightly unorthodox, yet have proven very effective. I think they'll help you too.

The standard advice is to take the club away as low as possible, either straight back from the ball or a bit inside the target line. My take-away is a little different from this; I actually start the club back slightly outside the target line rather than straight back. Also, fairly early in the take-away, I begin to "set," or cock, the wrists and right arm in a gradual, upward motion. This movement takes the clubhead up with it.

I believe this take-away movement, characterized by the clubhead moving a bit outside the target line and the wrists beginning to cock fairly early, helps you get into a position at the top of the swing that allows you to pull the club down freely and squarely along the target line. I'll explain why in a moment. For now, let's move on to the backswing.

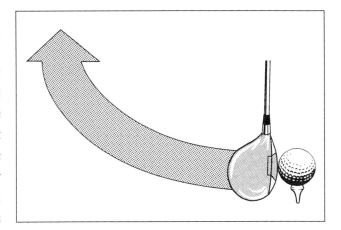

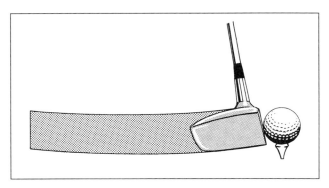

During my take-away, the club ascends quickly (top); this action, when timed correctly, enables me to return the club squarely along the target line in the impact zone (bottom).

As you continue back, make the fullest possible shoulder turn. Some of you will make a bigger turn than others, but virtually all of you can improve the degree you turn your shoulders on the backswing. You might not be able to match my shoulder turn, which is nearly 110 degrees with a driver. But if you can increase your turn from 70 to 80 degrees, you'll see a marked improvement in the distance and trajectory of your shots.

While my shoulders turn significantly, my hips turn only about thirty-five degrees. I generate much of my driving power from the tension that's built up between my upper and lower body because of my large shoulder turn and relatively small hip turn. But not everyone can do this. I recommend that you try to make as full a shoulder turn as possible and let the hips follow naturally. For most golfers, your hip turn will be about half the amount of your shoulder turn. As long as you're turning your shoulders fully, that's fine.

While my shoulders and hips turn around my spine in a relatively horizontal fashion, my arms swing the club on a more upright plane. (Actually, the difference between my arm and shoulder planes has become a little less noticeable in the last couple of years. My instructors, Paul Marchand and Dick Harmon, have advised me to stand a little farther from the ball than I used to. This makes my plane a little bit flatter and my path to the ball shallower, and it has helped.)

I believe in swinging the hands into a high position. Most amateurs swing the club too much around their bodies on a flat plane. Maybe it's because they've listened to the old advice that your right arm must remain tucked in to the right side at the top. Again, I feel this is too much of a restriction to a free-swinging motion. In my own swing, as well as those of Jack Nicklaus, Tom Watson, Seve Ballesteros, and a host of other champions, the arm swing is upright and the right elbow "flies" to some degree.

Like me, Seve Ballesteros (and other top champions) allows his right elbow to fly at the top of the backswing.

As the club moves to the top, you reach a crucial point in the swing. I know I've coached you to make as big an upper-body turn as you can. However, it must be a *stable* turn—your lower body must retain its position and you must stay in balance. A common error that occurs as the golfer approaches the top of the swing is to let the legs and hips sway to the right (for a right-handed player), rather than to resist and maintain a stable position. This, I believe, is the athletic part of the golf swing that everyone can improve up to a point, but some golfers will execute this better than others. To remain stable, focus on holding your right knee in the same spot that it was in at address. The more times you strive to do this, the easier it will become.

As I complete the backswing, my lower body is in a very stable position. In fact, my left heel has not risen at all. Not many golfers can make as big a turn as this without the left heel rising. But let me make it clear, it's fine if your left heel rises, as long as two conditions are met:

1. It rises because of the pull exerted on the upper body by the lower body.

2. It does not contribute to a sway to the right.

AT THE TOP: WHY CROSSING THE LINE IS OKAY

At the top of the driver backswing, the so-called ideal position is one in which the clubshaft is parallel to the target line. However, look at the accompanying photograph, and you'll see that my own club-shaft "crosses the line," i.e., points to the right of the target, by a good margin. Before I defend this position, I'd like to point out that recent magazine articles have shown that many top pros —including great swingers like Jack Nicklaus, Larry Mize, Greg

This is what the cross-the-line position looks like from directly overhead.

Norman, and Payne Stewart—cross the line on their long swing.

Why is this against-the-book characteristic evidenced in the swings of so many fine players? I believe it's a result of that more upright arm plane I mentioned earlier, in tandem with the big turns of today's players. Try the following experiment. Take a backswing with your right elbow tucked in tightly. Notice that the clubshaft points left of the target—in what's known as a "laid-off" position. Now swing your arms high and let your right elbow rise. You'll see that this action makes the club cross the line instead. When the club crosses the line, it gives you two advantages:

1. It lengthens the swing arc greatly, potentially giving you more power.

2. It makes it easy to start down from inside the target line (rather than throwing the club outside), which helps you deliver the club squarely into the ball and hit it accurately.

In my own case, from this crossing-the-line position, it's natural for me to drop the club inside the line I brought the club back on. Then, thanks to my slightly open body position, the club moves squarely down the target line through the ball. I never have to worry about cutting across the ball from outside-in. The worst I can expect is a slight push to the right. I can swing the club down with no last-second correction attempts. The time to get the right arm tight to the side is on the downswing—not the backswing. This dropping action of the hands and arms into a tightly wound downswing is what accounts for the massive power of many of today's Tour stars. It is much like the dropping action of the bat of many of the great baseball swingers like my friend George Brett. More on that in a moment.

To summarize my key objectives during the backswing: I take the club away slightly outside the target line; swing the hands as I get my wrists and right arm cocked on an upright plane; and let the right arm and shoulder rise at the top of the backswing, so that the club crosses the line slightly. This combination of movements makes it easy to just unwind on the downswing, so you bring the clubhead from inside to along the target line. I believe you too will find you can develop these positions while encompassing them into a smooth-flowing action. Remember, loose arms and big shoulder turn.

One last point regarding the top-of-swing position: my left wrist is slightly concave, or "cupped," at the top. Many professional golfers will advocate a flat position of the left wrist, because it indicates that the clubface is also square in relation to the arc of the swing. The cupped position at the top means the clubface is slightly open, whereas a "bowed" wrist position means the clubface will be relatively closed at the top. (The driver clubface is open at the top if the toe is pointing down, it's closed if it's pointing more or less at the sky, and it's square if it's midway between the two positions.)

It's okay if your left wrist is flat and your clubface is square at the top. I prefer the slightly cupped position, which indicates a slightly open clubface, because I know that on the downswing I can really let my wrists whip into the ball with no fear of hitting a wild hook. I think, therefore, that the cupped position ultimately results in a more powerful golf shot.

If you tend to hook the ball off target, this cupped position at the top could help remedy your problem.

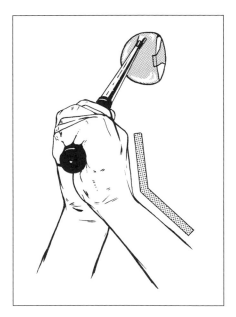

Although there have been several great players who swing from a bowed left wrist position at the top, I believe most players who attempt this are constantly fighting the clubhead release, trying to hold the clubface from closing too much at impact. Ultimately, this results in loss of both direction and power.

Practice your backswing in front of a full-length mirror. Try to incorporate all the points mentioned and also try to make sure your left wrist is either square or slightly cupped at the top. These rehearsals will stand you in good stead out on the course.

THE DOWNSWING: SHIFT, DROP, RELEASE

To me, when hitting the long clubs, the downswing is the simplest part of the game. That's because the downswing happens so quickly that you can't possibly think your way through it. The best downswing is almost totally a reflexive, reactive move. It's a result of what you established through a sound, yet relaxed, setup position, a smooth, complete coiling action of the body during the backswing, and the loose hinging of the right arm and wrists.

Ironically, many club-level golfers struggle with the downswing because they try so hard to create speed that they ruin the swing of the club. Don't you, or else you'll strike the ball with a glancing blow and with the clubface open, hitting a bad push or slice. I want you to swing freely through the ball and release the club around your body with abandon.

You must release the club fully to obtain maximum clubhead speed and consistent clubhead delivery. Therefore, I suggest you think of three words to use as guides for your downswing: *shift, drop,* and *release.* Some of you may find you'll need to emphasize one of these thoughts more than the other two to deliver the club squarely and powerfully into the ball at impact. Please understand that this downswing action occurs in an utter flash. I don't want to make this explanation any harder for you than I have to. Picture my descriptions in your mind a few times and then take lots of practice swings without a ball. I think over time you can become like me and swing with virtually no swing thoughts at all. I know I play my best when I really just "feel" my swing and let it happen in a fluid, aggressive manner. For now, let's make sure you understand what these moves are.

Shift

For the right-handed player, the shift refers to a smooth movement of the weight from the right foot at the top of the backswing, onto the left foot to start the downswing. Notice my emphasis on tempo. Most amateurs know they're supposed to shift their weight onto their left foot. The trouble is that many of them overdo it. Instead of a smooth transition, they make what I call a hard drive toward the target. This is a lurching lateral move that actually prevents the body rotation and clubhead release from occurring with proper timing through the impact zone. So, although you definitely should shift your weight from the right foot to the left, it must be a smooth move, so the body stays poised and balanced. It's not a big move. I would describe it as a slight lateral motion toward the target with your hips, followed by a turn to the left of the hips.

Drop

This is a really obvious movement in my swing and it should be in yours. Blended into, but momentarily following, the shift to the left, your right arm (that is high in the sky at the top) quickly but smoothly drops to your side. As this happens your

The shift position (above). The drop position (below).

right arm and wrists stay cocked and the butt end of the club descends toward the ball with no hint of a hit or strike. It's important to note that this movement is coordinated with the shift, and is largely a movement of your arms—not your right shoulder. You can practice this move by keeping your shoulders turned and just letting your club and arms fall straight down. Do it several times daily, from the top of the swing down, then back up. You'll quickly feel why having loose arms is so important. If you can get this into your swing it will leave you loaded with power.

Release

This is the fun part of the swing. I truly believe that this next series of moves is what to a large degree accounts for my strong ball flight and day-to-day consistency of flush contact. Think about the release and practice it over and over.

Imagine the clubhead flying around your body up and to the left as if on a circular rollercoaster, with no time to stop for the ball. To accomplish this, your left arm (which has been straight all this time) will fold or bend at the elbow closely to your left side. Your right arm (which has been cocked) now straightens through and past the ball. Your wrists (which were cocked deep into your downswing) now quickly uncock and recock so that the butt end of the club (which was pointing behind the ball at the ground) is now pointing at the ground in front of where the ball was. As this hinge motion takes place your hips and shoulders swivel around the spine angle that you had at address. You'll notice in the photographs of my swing that this continuous rotation carries me way around to the left so that the club very comfortably ends up on my left shoulder. It's the very circular motion of my swivel and the clubhead up and to the left that takes me there.

One last note on the release: I feel a very coordinated relationship between the shift and rotation of my body and the whiplike hinge motion in my arms and wrists. At times my reactions are so good that I feel I can snap the clubhead off the end of my shaft through the impact area with my aggressive releasing motion. It's ironic that under pressure it's this free relasing that I rely on to hit accurate, strong shots—instead of obvious overcontrol that I see so often in Wednesday pro-ams. Let's agree that from now on you'll work to be smooth and let the clubhead fly. Overcontrolling the ball and early exertion of the upper body to hit turns golf into a frustrating ball hunt.

Let's review what the result of these motions is. By allowing the right arm to swing away from the body at the top of the backswing, the club can approach the ball from inside the target line, eliminating any impulse to hit "at" the ball with your right arm and shoulder, a destructive move that throws the club outside the target line and contributes to that severe slice. As I've mentioned earlier, I actually

The classic release position.

drop or loop the club a little bit to the inside of the arc described by the club on the backswing. Because of my big shoulder rotation and right arm freedom, I tend to come into the ball from the inside, and I would actually push most of my shots to the right if I lined up dead square to the target. That's why I line up slightly left of target at address—it allows me to release the club straight down the target line and around to the left. Thus my normal shot flies almost dead straight, only fading slightly right in the air.

You may find that you don't drop your arms and hands as much to the inside as I do. That's fine, as long as you don't make that right shoulder hitting move that throws the clubhead outside the target line and causes you to cut across the ball. If you find that your natural release brings the clubhead through the ball consistently square to the target line, that's great. All you need to do is align as squarely as possible at address for unfailingly straight, powerfully hit shots.

POSTIMPACT:
A REFLECTION OF THE SWING ITSELF

You can't fake a good follow-through. You also can't improve your shots by posing in a pretty finish that's disconnected from the actions that preceded it. That won't help you; the ball's already gone and all you can do is talk to it.

A natural, well-balanced follow-through and finish will be yours if you set up correctly, coil fully around your spine on the backswing, uncoil around it on the downswing, maintain your balance, and hinge your arms and the club fluidly through the ball. You can use your own postimpact positions as checkpoints for what actually occurred during your swing. Here's how.

The Follow-through

At a point beyond impact, when you arrive in the classic "early follow-through" position, your right arm should be fully extended. If your right arm is not fully extended, it means you hit with your shoulders. In other words, you were holding the club up through the impact zone, not releasing it. The butt end of the clubshaft should be pointing at the ground and your hips and shoulders should be rotated around your spine angle to the left.

As you reach the complete follow-through, your entire chest, midsection, and hips should point directly at or even left of the target. If you're not in this position, you neglected to rotate your entire body during the downswing. It also proves that you didn't make a full body coil on the backswing, and the timing of the reaction between your body and arms was poor. Think of the big circle on the left side of your body and let your left arm fold.

The Finish

In the finish position, almost all of your weight should be planted solidly on your left foot and you should be up on a pointed right toe. If you find you're back on your right foot rather than up on your right toe, you know that you didn't execute your initial shift and/or your circular body rotation, thus you hung back on your right foot.

The club should be dangling at an angle behind your left shoulder. Both arms should be bent slightly at the elbows. Your hands should be just above your left shoulder. Many handicap players finish with their arms extended stiffly, so the club is pointing either at the target or up to the sky. Such a position tells you there was an extreme amount of upper body and arm tension throughout the swinging action. It suggests a need to review your address posture to make sure that you're gripping the club very lightly and allowing your arms to hang down loosely from your shoulders, rather than extending them stiffly outward.

The classic finish position.

COUPLES'S CLINIC

1 POWER PLAYS

In this chapter I've emphasized the need to develop your personal maximum shoulder and upper-body turn. This is the basis for increasing the speed you can generate at impact and the distance you can hit the ball, then understanding how that sets up the best possible positioning for a free and powerful swing through the ball. Practice the shift, drop, release often. You too can enjoy the freedom and power of putting your reactions and coordination in your swing. No more fear and tension, right?

That said, I'd like to add this thought: while you want to make as full a turn as you can, remember that you must do it within the framework of balance. Therefore, I suggest that in most cases during play you leave just a fraction of your shoulder turn—and your power—"in the bag," in the interests of maintaining poise and keeping the ball in play.

However, there are usually several holes on every course that may invite you to make a power play. These are either long par-four or par-five holes in which there's plenty of room off the tee but where you need your Sunday punch to reach the long par four in regulation or perhaps the par five in two. In these situations only, go ahead and reach back for your absolute maximum upper-body turn and full-throttle release.

If anything, try to swing the club back more smoothly than usual. Give yourself an extra split second at the top before you begin a full, free unwind and release through the ball. Finally, remember to keep your head behind the ball's position until after impact. Swivel around your spine angle and enjoy a free swing through to the finish.

2 BACK ON TRACK

In my address for the driver and other long clubs, my hands are positioned slightly behind the ball. Many top pros advocate that the hands be positioned slightly farther forward. However, I think my hand position at address offers a couple of benefits that will prove worthwhile to you.

1. With your hands in this position, you're more likely to move the club away from the ball *slowly.* The first move must be a gentle push back with the hands and arms, blended into a full shoulder rotation to the top (rather than an abrupt pickup with the wrists, which is likely when you start with your hands ahead of the ball).

2. By starting from this position, you'll find it's easier to start the club back from the ball a touch outside the target line or at least square to the target line. If you start the swing with your hands ahead of the ball, the natural tendency will be to draw the clubhead inside the target line immediately. As we've discussed, this is the start of a too-flat arm swing going back, which usually causes the common right shoulder from the top downswing. The result: a dreaded slice, push, or pull hook shot.

So, a starting position with your hands a shade behind the ball can help put your backswing back on track.

3 INCH IT UP

On drives, I play the ball a shade more forward in my stance than most club-level golfers. Playing the ball up will give you the maximum forward thrust and thus distance on your tee shots. Here's why: you'll contact it as the driver clubhead has passed its lowest point and is beginning its upswing. Keep in mind that an average driver carries about ten degrees of loft on its face. If you've teed the ball fairly high as I suggested, you're in a position to contact the ball with the clubface moving upward by several degrees from horizontal, in other words, so that the forward thrust is virtually at right angles to the ten degrees or so of loft on the clubface. This is the flushest, most powerful delivery of the clubhead to the ball you can make.

So, with the driver, inch up your ball position to set up that powerful sweeping hit. With good execution, the result will be a pro-level trajectory—a driving, parabolic flight that provides maximum carry and, because little backspin is applied, extra roll upon landing.

4 ROOM FOR IMPROVEMENT

You want your body to be tension free at address. Moreover, you want a setup position that gives your hands and arms enough room to extend through the impact zone, rather than be cramped so you feel like you're trying to steer the clubhead through the ball.

To accomplish these technical goals, bend a shade more from the waist, about twenty degrees, so your arms hang straight down in a relaxed fashion, about six inches away from your body.

5 EASY DOES IT

Most handicap players lack confidence in (or maybe it's accurate to say they fear) the long irons. While it's true that good technique is essential for good long-iron play, tempo is an important element too.

You'll rarely see a fine player hit a strong, straight long-iron shot with a quick, jumpy swing action. Most great long-iron players take the club back very slowly from the ball and maintain an extrasmooth tempo the whole way. This is essential with the long irons, more than with any other club. The tendency is to think you have to do something extra during the swing with the long irons to hit the ball powerfully. Just the opposite is true. Give yourself plenty of time on the backswing to generate a nice full upper-body coil, then smoothly combine the downswing keys of shift-drop-release. Make sure to swing around a constant spine angle, and you'll be pleasantly surprised at how well you can strike the long irons.

6 UPRIGHT OR FLAT?

The plane of your golf swing will be determined somewhat by your height (as well as the length of club you're swinging). Given the limits of your physical stature, I recommend that you practice developing a slightly more upright rather than a flat swing plane. The main reason is:

An upright arm swing builds more power. You can make the clubhead travel in a longer arc by reaching for the sky instead of swinging the club more horizontally around you and keeping your hands low. The key is still to have a circular motion with the hands high at the top.

Remember to start the clubhead back and, if anything, slightly outside the target line. Then, as your shoulders turn, reach high with your hands so the clubhead describes a fairly upright swing plane.

7 LOOP-DE-LOOP

In the start-down position of the downswing, my arms, my hands, and the club move to a position on the *inside* of the point I reached at the top of my backswing. I have, in effect, "looped" the club slightly inside the arc it took on the backswing. This is a move I share with several other top players—Lee Trevino foremost among them.

Because this loop-de-loop action is insurance against throwing the club outside with the right shoulder on the downswing (probably the most common flaw of amateur golfers), you might want to try grooving it in practice. This is the only time you can consciously stop and freeze this downswing position. Out on the course, you can't stop at the top, think out your downswing, then deliver the club into the ball. The entire swing must be one uninterrupted motion that flows.

8 TO LIFT OR NOT TO LIFT

As I mentioned earlier, I keep my left heel planted firmly on the ground at the top of a full backswing, even when I use a driver. Does this mean I think you should do the same? Not necessarily. In fact, you might have to *let* your left heel lift to get enough backswing rotation, and to let all the good things that I've already mentioned happen on the downswing.

Notice that I did not say that you should consciously lift your heel. The left heel rises solely as a response to the clockwise turn you generate with your body. When most golfers make their fullest shoulder turn, their hips will also turn quite a bit; when this happens, their left heel is pulled off the ground. As long as you retain good balance with most of your weight solidly on your right foot, this is fine.

As mentioned, I happen to have unusual suppleness, so that I can make a big shoulder turn without my hips turning very much at all. Therefore, my left heel is not pulled upward.

Again, as long as you're in balance and the left heel rises as a response to your body turn, lifting the heel a little is fine. The point is that your shoulders lead your hips on the backswing to ensure a coiling action that will allow for the shift, drop, and release.

9 REVERSE PIVOT REMEDIES

A common fault among handicap players is a reverse pivot—a move in which the right-handed player keeps his or her weight on the left side during the backswing, then shifts it to the right during the downswing. The result is usually either a weak, looping shot or a fat shot in which the clubhead strikes the ground behind the ball.

Here are several keys that can help you shift your weight properly:

1. *Extend your take-away fully.* Push the club straight back from the ball. This initiates a wide swing arc, in which your weight will also begin to flow from the left foot to the right.

2. *Turn your left shoulder under your chin.* Some golfers make a "false" turn in which the left shoulder never gets by the chin, thus restricting the shoulder turn. When the turn is restricted, so is the weight shift; and it creates a tilting motion with no coil. Learn to keep your chin slightly up at address so that your left shoulder can keep moving beneath it smoothly.

3. *Move over to the right.* Consciously feel your weight move to the inside of your right foot and leg as you make your rotation to the top of your backswing.

4. *Turn your shoulders at a right angle to your spine.* For most, it will feel like a horizontal rotation of the upper body instead of a dipping or tilting of the shoulders.

10 ALL TOGETHER NOW

As you probably understand by now, I'm a bear about the importance of maintaining an even swing tempo and not hitting at the ball. Yet, we've all run into periods during which we lose our rhythm, usually because we've unconsciously (or consciously) tried to hit the ball too hard, or because the timing of the reaction just isn't there. If you realize you've lost your best swing rhythm, this simple practice routine will help get your tempo back on track.

1. First, hit about a dozen seven-iron shots with your normal swing.
2. Next, take out your driver, tee the ball up, and hit it the same distance as your normal seven-iron. Yes, that's right. Hit your driver that specific short distance with eight or ten balls.
3. Hit about a dozen five-iron shots with your normal swing to determine your normal distance.
4. Hit eight to ten shots with your driver the same distance as your normal five-iron shot.
5. Hit a dozen of your normal three-iron shots.
6. Again, hit some balls with the driver the same distance as your normal three-iron shot.
7. Finally, finish the session by hitting some really smooth shots with your driver. By this time you should be swinging with a beautiful rhythm and even tempo.

Remember: the best rule for finding your ideal tempo is to learn to swing the club at the maximum speed at which you feel the best timing between your body, your arms, and the club-head. This drill will help you truly feel that timing.

11 GROOVE GOOD POSITIONS

Although there's no substitute for constant repetition of the swing while actually hitting balls, you can still improve your technique when you're indoors by mimicking these three positions in front of a full-length mirror as often as you can (without hitting a single shot).

1. *A tension-free address.* Step up to the ball, taking a stance of comfortable width with both toes pointed out slightly. You should have just a subtle flex in the knees, a moderate bend from the waist with your arms hanging down loosely into your grip position, and the weight distributed equally between both feet and favoring the insides. Your spine (the axis of your rotation) should be leaning straight forward.

2. *Coil to the top.* Practice pushing the club immediately back with your left shoulder and arm, slightly outside the target line; then gradually setting the wrists and right arm about halfway through the backswing. Continue to turn your shoulders as far as you can while shifting your weight to the inside of a braced right leg. Feel your back and shoulders stretch. Reach for the sky.

3. *Shift, drop, and release.* All in one motion, shift your weight smoothly onto your left foot; drop your arms, keeping the club cocked; and loosely uncock and recock your arms and wrists around to the left, so that you have a full uncoil of your hips and shoulders, and the club rests gently on your left shoulder.

12 JITTER-PROOF

Several pros will admit (at least privately) to having frequent cases of the jitters before teeing off on the first hole. I'm one who will freely admit to this, particularly at one of the four major championships. If we pros who make our living swinging the club are prone to first-tee jitters, it stands to reason that it's even tougher for you, the weekend player who's not nearly as prepared.

Here are two tips that will work wonders for your confidence on the first tee.

1. Hit some warmup shots before you play. Even if you hit only a dozen balls, it will help to get the feel of the clubface and ball meeting, especially if you haven't played for a week or more. Make it a habit to get to the course thirty minutes early, so you can at least hit a few full shots, chips, and putts. Focus on the rhythm of your movements and the looseness in your arms. Honestly, don't worry about where the ball goes. Think about getting your "feel" warmed up.

2. Once on the first tee, imagine you're still on the wide-open practice tee you just left. Take a few deep breaths; then simply go ahead and make the same *carefree* swing you made just a few minutes before. You'll be pleasantly surprised at how often this little mental gimmick will help you make extra-good contact and zip one down the middle.

13 MY SECRET WEAPON

I carry a club that has been my secret weapon over the past couple of years. It's a three-wood (or three-metal) that I borrowed from Tom Watson a while back. I hit it so well, I conveniently "forgot" to give it back. But Tom understands. When you find a club that seems made for you, few Tour players would demand that you give it back.

This particular club is a strong three-wood, having just thirteen degrees of loft. I've found it's fantastic, because with this lower loft, I can hit it a good 260 yards off the fairway. Thus it has extended the range of par-five holes I can reach in two.

More important, I've found this club to be great off the tee on medium-length par-four holes for which accuracy is an important factor. I can hit a teed-up ball about 270 yards with it under normal conditions, just ten to fifteen yards shorter than I hit the driver.

My point is not to tell you to use exactly the same club as I do. Rather, it's to suggest you look for that "tweener" type of club—one that you can hit off the fairway effectively yet can also be your ace in the hole when you have to hit it in the fairway off the tee. For you, this may be a club with fifteen, sixteen, or seventeen degrees of loft. That's not what matters. What matters is that once you feel your swing has gained consistency, you will have a club you know will put the ball into play with reasonable distance and will give you great confidence.

14 PICK YOUR STICK

I'd like to describe the characteristics of the driver I use, perhaps to debunk a few myths and to give you a starting point toward what you should consider when picking your stick.

I use a driver made by Lynx, the company I represent, that has the following specifications:

| Length | 43$\frac{1}{2}$ inches |
| Loft | 9 degrees |

Lie	1 degree upright
Swing weight	D-4
Shaft material	Steel
Shaft flex	x-100 (tipped one inch)
Grip size	$^{1}/_{32}$ inch oversize

If you know a little about clubs, you can tell that this driver is not outrageously different from the one you might use. The standard driver length for the majority of manufacturers today is $43^{1}/_{2}$ inches. My clubface loft, nine degrees, is about the average used on the PGA Tour. My swing weight of D-4 is a shade heavier than average for a men's driver. And the flex specification of x-100 means the club is a fairly stiff shaft because of my high clubhead speed. Let me add that there are definitely stiffer driver shafts being used on the Tour. Finally, the slightly oversize grip simply suits my hand size. Especially since I don't wear a glove.

I just wanted you to know that although I'm one of the longest drivers on the PGA Tour, I don't use a club with particularly outlandish "power hitter" specifications. The moral: when you're selecting a driver (or any club), go with the specs that are *most playable for you.* Leave the ego trips to the players who aren't as smart; you'll be on the winning end of a lot more matches.

3 | THE SHORT SWING

Direction, Not Distance, Is the Priority

The next goal of this book is to assist in lowering your scores by helping you to understand and apply the principles of the short swing. When I speak of the short swing, I'm referring to your "scoring" shots—the strokes you'll play with the seven-, eight-, and nine-irons and the wedges. This chapter will discuss not only the full shots with these clubs but also half and three-quarter shots played from fifty to one hundred yards.

A MIND-SET ADJUSTMENT

I think it's important for all golfers to understand that as they get within a closer range of the flagstick, their outlook on what they're trying to accomplish changes somewhat. Now, more than with the longer clubs, accuracy is the focal point.

Remember, off the tee you're hitting your driver toward an "area," that is, the fairway, rather than to a single precise spot on the fairway. If you're driving well, you might even expect to hit one side of the fairway or the other, for better position on your approach shot. Still, off the tee you're not trying to limit your distance to reach a certain spot; the longer you can hit it, generally, the better. Likewise, with the fairway metals or long irons, you're striving to make square, solid contact in which (assuming it's in range) your target is the green.

At some point, though, all golfers should recognize the distance at which they begin to focus on the precise target, which is the flag itself. This is the spot to which you're expecting to get the ball as close as possible to set up a birdie effort. At this range, your short, or "accuracy," swing takes precedence. I've suggested that this mind-set might take over from the seven-iron on in. The club and distance range from the flag might vary from one player to the next, but the mind-set shouldn't. The first thing I'd like to suggest is that you should rarely, if ever, take a hard, full swing with the shorter irons. Always take enough club so that there's no question that you can hit the ball "up" to the hole with a controlled swing action.

You know, it's funny how many amateurs, particularly lower handicappers who should know better, try to force a shot to the hole with a given club, when it would be so much easier to just take more club. I think it's because a lot of golfers like to brag about what club they hit to the green on a certain hole. For example, a club player might brag that on a 420-yard par four, he hit a wedge onto the green. The professional would not be impressed by this; he or she would ask, "Well, what did you score on the hole?" That's all that really matters.

One of the masters at taking plenty of club and then making a disciplined swing that keeps the ball under control for both line and distance is Hale Irwin. Hale will often take one more club, sometimes two more, than his playing partners, but he sure is hard to beat getting irons close to the hole. That (along with his straight driving) is the reason Hale has won three U.S. Opens, including his 1990 victory over my good friend Mike Donald.

Always take enough club to hit a controlled short-iron approach—regardless of what other members of your foursome select.

Now let's talk about the setup and swing adjustments needed to help you get the ball close. The two differences that you're trying to produce in the short swing are

1. A somewhat narrower, more controlled swing arc
2. A slightly more descending clubhead path through the ball

This slightly descending path puts backspin on the ball for optimum control of the shot. Note that I said a *slightly* descending path. The goal is to produce short-iron shots that land softly and stop quickly. You do *not* have to dig down deeply and gouge out

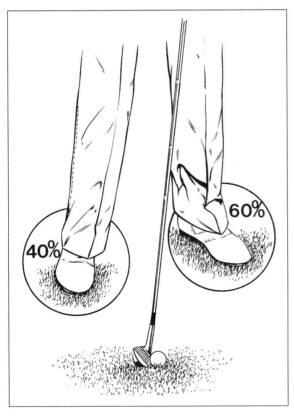

Putting 60 percent of your weight on your left foot is one of the most important principles of the short-swing setup.

huge divots to hit a quick-stopping shot. In fact, some pros such as Greg Norman have discovered that by hitting down too sharply and powerfully, they put too much backspin on the ball. In the last year or two, Greg has softened his approach to the short-iron swing, hitting down on these shots less sharply and swinging with less speed. I believe Greg has become an even better player for it.

At any rate, there are five specific setup adjustments you should make when moving from the long swing to attacking the flag with the short iron. They are described below.

1. *Put more weight on your left side.* Whereas you might favor a fifty-fifty weight distribution at address with the long clubs, you should put 60 percent of your weight on your left, or forward, foot when setting up to play a typical short iron or wedge shot. Your head will also be over, rather than behind, the ball. This simple adjustment ensures that your downswing arc will be a bit steeper than for the long clubs, with no conscious swing adjustment on your part.

2. *Move the ball back slightly in the stance.* When playing any of the short clubs, position the ball about two inches back from a spot opposite your left heel. Note that your stance will be getting narrower as the length of shot decreases. This, plus the fact that the ball is a little farther back, actually puts the ball just ahead of the center of the stance. This ball position also acts to guarantee the ball-first contact you need for these shots.

3. *Place your hands just ahead of the ball.* Basically, you'll position your hands at address in relation to your body the same way you would for the long clubs. However, because the ball is a bit farther back in your stance, your hands will now be positioned slightly ahead of the ball.

4. *Square your right foot to the target line.* In Chapter 2, I asked you to "toe out" both feet as a means of encouraging as full a backswing and downswing turn as possible. When you're moving into the short-swing zone, however, stability over the ball should take precedence over the degree of turn and the power generated. For this reason, you should turn your right or rear foot in a bit, so that it's nearly perpendicular to the target line. This will slightly curtail your body turn and thus your backswing turn, but it will add control to your swing arc.

5. *Open your stance slightly.* The shorter the shot, the more open your stance should be compared with your long-swing alignment. There are two reasons for this. First, it's easier to get a good visualization of your target from a somewhat open position. Second, which I've never heard mentioned before but which is significant to me, is this: with the ball a little farther back in your stance, the clubface doesn't have quite as much time to get squared up at the point of impact. (Or you could say impact occurs a little "earlier.") For this reason, if you were aligned dead square to the target, the clubface would tend to be just a fraction open at impact for the short swing. By opening your stance and body line a bit, you're effectively allowing yourself to bring the clubface into the ball right along the target line.

THE SHORT-SWING BACKSWING

In terms of the swing itself, there's very little difference between the motion made with the long clubs and the short clubs. Because you're now focusing on hitting the ball a precise distance as well as on a precise line, you'll simply be making a swing that's a more compact and a little more controlled than the one I described previously. And the minor setup changes I've introduced will, to a large extent, make this compact backswing *automatic.*

Keep in mind that once you get within the yardage range of a full swing with your wedges, you'll need to practice so you can feel how much you need to limit your

Good short-iron play demands that you make a compact swing.

backswing to produce the required distance. Depending on your personal swing strength (as well as the loft on your wedges), this distance may be from ninety yards to seventy-five yards to sixty yards—more on that later.

Let's review the movements in the short-swing backswing. First, as you push the clubhead back from the ball, you should almost immediately begin to set, or cock, your wrists and right arm, so the clubhead begins to rise up from the ground more quickly than with the longer clubs. For the shorter clubs, I'd say this upward cocking of your wrists and right arm should begin as your hands pass your right knee. This earlier set will help you keep the swing compact and allow you to execute your backswing turn over the ball with less chance of swaying off balance.

Continue swinging the hands and arms on an upright plane. Actually, this adjusted backswing plane will be pretty much taken care of by a correct setup posture. You should have the slight bend from the waist with your arms hanging freely. However, since a short-iron or wedge clubshaft is quite a bit shorter, you'll be standing closer to the ball at address than you would with a driver or three-wood. Because of this, your swing should automatically become more upright. Just make sure to work your left shoulder under your chin and reach your hands toward the sky as you continue to turn around your spine.

A third point regarding the short-swing backswing is to keep the right knee firmly in its original position. If anything, this is even more crucial here than in the long swing. Never let the right knee buckle outward on a shorter shot. This fault changes the arc of your swing so that it's wide rather than narrow. Moreover, it causes your upper body to move laterally with it, which makes clubface-to-ball contact more chancy.

A little lateral sway on a tee shot might not hurt you too much, but it becomes a bigger problem on the short swings. Why? Because the wider arc that accompanies that sway can cause the clubhead to catch some grass between clubface and ball. Getting grass between clubface and ball produces a "flier," in which the ball carries and rolls ten to twenty yards farther than it would have with clean contact. And if you're planning to hit a shot 120 yards to the stick, it can be disastrous if you hit it 130 or 140 instead. So keep the right knee firm, with the weight on the inside of your right foot, as you reach toward the top.

Finally, make sure to keep your tempo brisk. This more compact, firmer swing action is still smooth, but slightly more upbeat than the long flowing swing used for the distance shots. Remember, this is a stroke in which control is crucial.

DOWN AND THROUGH ON THE SHORT SWING

You're at the top, in position to deliver a nicely controlled, descending blow to the golf ball. Because you started with a little more weight on your left side, your stance was slightly narrower, and you kept your right knee braced to the inside, you should be in a very stable position over the ball, with most of your weight on the inside of your right leg. Because your right foot was pointed perpendicular to the target line at address, your backswing turn has been restricted somewhat. So the short-iron clubshaft probably will not reach a position parallel to the ground (the swings of golfers like John Daly are exceptions to that rule). Furthermore, since your turn was slightly less extreme, your left heel was less likely to have been pulled off the ground as it might have been in the long swing.

From this point, all you have to do is very smoothly move your weight onto your left side. In fact, as the length of the shot decreases, you should sense that your arm swing is becoming a little more aggressive while your lower body weight shift is becoming less pronounced.

As you begin to shift and turn your body through the shot, pull down a little more aggressively with the left hand and arm. You want to have the feeling on the short swings that the back of the left hand is leading the clubhead down and through the ball. In fact, it may help you to think of the clubface as an extension of the back of your left hand. Just pull that hand down and through while keeping your head still.

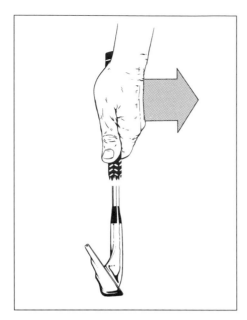

When playing a short-iron shot, you want to feel that the back of your left hand leads the club into the ball.

On standard short-iron shots, the club should contact the ball just before it reaches its lowest point.

Because you've located the ball two or three inches farther back in your stance than for your long swing, you should contact the ball just before the clubhead reaches its lowest point. This correct descending blow makes the clubface "grip" the ball for a split second; it then rolls up the lofted clubface somewhat before actually leaving it with a backward rotation—with backspin—which will help it hold its line and stop quickly after landing.

Meanwhile, the clubhead should nip the turf after contact with the ball. Depending on the firmness of the ground, you may or may not take a small divot. *Note:* I don't think any player should consciously strive to take a large divot on short-iron and pitch shots. Some amateurs seem to believe that a big divot is necessary. It's not. I've found that if you try to smash down and take a big divot, you'll jerk the club down rather than swing it, usually causing a mis-hit shot (most often a fat shot). So all you need to do is pull your left arm through the shot and keep your circular body turn moving through impact.

Your finish on the short swing should be relaxed and natural, very similar to the one I described for the long swing. Your body should face the target with your weight predominantly on your left foot. With the short swing, your finish will be slightly briefer than with the long swing, for two reasons. First, the percentage of your weight shifted back and through the shot is slightly less than for the long clubs. Second, because you made a firmer, more compact motion, the releasing action is not as loose or as full. The wrist "recock" and the left arm "fold" are not as pronounced as with the longer clubs. This too will serve to abbreviate the follow-through a bit.

Remember, the key point in any good follow-through is *balance.*

PITCHOUTS: TWO SURE WAYS TO MAKE PAR (OR BIRDIE) FROM FIFTY TO ONE HUNDRED YARDS

At this point, let's get into a little more detail about how to produce the little half and three-quarter wedge shots that are vital to good scoring at any level. Stop and think about how many shots you play that are longer than a greenside chip, yet shorter than one hundred yards from the flag. Often, if you've hit a poor drive and been forced to play out from trouble, you'll need a fine shot from fifty to one

At the completion of the short swing, you should feel very balanced and poised.

hundred yards to have a chance to make par. Alternatively, two good shots on a par five or a booming tee shot on a short par four may leave you in the range in which you should be able to give yourself a good crack at a birdie.

There are endless adjustments that can be made in the setup and stroke techniques to fit the precise requirements of the distance, ground condition, and pin position at hand. But basically, these partial shots fall into two categories: the soft pitch and the pitch-and-run.

The Soft Pitch

The soft pitch is a must in situations in which the pin is toward the front of the green, so you have little landing area to work with. It's

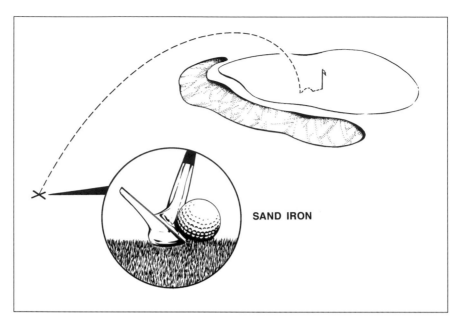

The soft pitch is the ideal shot to hit when you must carry a bunker and stop the ball quickly.

particularly useful when the pin is also closely guarded by a bunker. Here, you must hit a shot that drops to the green at a steep angle while also carrying some backspin, so it will stop very quickly, or dead, after just one soft bounce.

For this shot, go with your sand wedge or your third or *L*-wedge if you carry one. The *L*-wedge can be most effective in situations when the green is very firm and fast, because it has the greatest loft (usually between fifty-eight and sixty-two degrees). Also, since it has a smaller flange than a sand wedge, there's less chance of blading the shot, especially if the lie is tight. *Note:* Make sure the shot distance is within comfortable range of whichever club you choose. You should never force the short pitch.

Once you've selected your club, you should make the following setup adjustments to your normal short-iron swing.

1. *Even weight distribution.* Your weight should be balanced about fifty-fifty between the feet. This will help you make use of the full loft of your sand or *L*-wedge to throw the shot high into the air. Your stance should, as usual, be fairly narrow and quite open for this shot.

2. *Forward ball position.* The ball should be in a forward position, opposite your left heel, for the soft pitch. This will allow you to catch the ball at the bottom of your swing arc, again promoting the highest, softest shot possible.

3. *Slightly open clubface with alignment to the left.* Unlike most situations when you set the clubface square to the target, you should open your clubface slightly at address. You should also aim left in the same proportion that you open the clubface.

4. *Hands level with the ball.* Your hand position is a function of your ball position. Because you've moved the ball farther up in your stance than for other short shots, your hands should be level with the ball, or just a touch behind it, rather than leading.

Once you've made these setup adjustments, I have good news for you. The swing action that we have gone over for the full swing is ideal for this type of shot. Over the years, I have found that my free rotation and lazy and looping arm swing really lends itself to these types of soft pitch shots as well as bunker shots. If you get used to aligning your body left and opening the clubface, then use a very loose wrist and arm action to play soft pitches. The looping under on the downswing allows you to get such a shallow path of the clubhead through the ball that it feels like you're hitting up on it. In fact, if you brush the grass just behind the ball, it will fly high and come down soft every time.

I'd like to give you two pieces of advice I think are very important when playing the soft pitch with the sand or *L*-wedge.

1. In general, make a fuller swing than you might think you'll need. This is wise because you've opened the clubface slightly and are playing the ball more forward in your stance than you would in a basic pitch. Because more energy is being imparted to make the ball go up, the ball won't go quite as far forward as you may think.

Also, the reason you're playing this type of shot in the first place is to loft it over a bunker or deep rough. So, at least in the early stages, if you face a soft pitch shot of sixty yards, make a swing that feels as if you'll hit it seventy to seventy-five yards. This will ensure that you won't experience that sensation of having hit the shot just right, yet having it fall short in the bunker. The more you practice, the more feel for distance you'll develop on this shot. For starters, though, make sure you take too much swing, if anything.

2. Play the soft pitch only from fairly soft fairway lies or good lies in light rough. You need a good lie to use the setup and swing adjustments described, while at the same time making sure you get the club's leading edge under the ball at impact.

What if you face a shot that calls for the soft pitch to get close and you have drawn a tight lie? I suggest that until you've developed great confidence in the shot, you'll be better off making a basic short-swing pitch with the pitching wedge instead of the sand wedge so the club won't bounce off the hard turf. The shot won't fly as high or stop as softly near the flag, but sometimes it pays to play the percentages. This is one of those situations.

The Pitch-and-run

The pitch-and-run is a partial shot that's basically the opposite of the soft pitch. Here, you want to hit a lower-than-normal shot that will run, or release, rather than stop quickly on landing. Shot situations calling for the pitch-and-run include the following:

- When the shot is either into or against a strong wind, so that a lower flight provides more control
- Either when the green is open in front, so you can run the ball on, or the pin is placed toward the back of a long green, so there's plenty of green to work with
- Whenever the pin is on the back of a tiered green and a high pitch carrying all the way to the hole won't hold at the top tier

■ When the lie is tight with sparse or no grass, so that a lofted pitch is risky

The pitch-and-run can normally be played from anywhere up to about one hundred yards out. Depending on conditions, the pitch-and-run can be played with any number of clubs, from a seven-iron all the way through the sand or *L*-wedge. Most commonly, I'll play the shot with either a nine-iron or pitching wedge. Generally speaking, you should use a less-lofted club if the shot's into the wind and go with one of the wedges when the shot is downwind and/or the ground is extra firm.

As to the stroke for the pitch-and-run, you should make the following adjustments to your normal short-iron swing.

1. *Forward weight distribution.* Place about 70 percent of your weight on your left foot at address; more than for any other short swing.
2. *Ball back in stance, hands ahead.* The ball should be centered, or just behind center, and you should be in a fairly narrow, squared stance. With this ball position, your hands

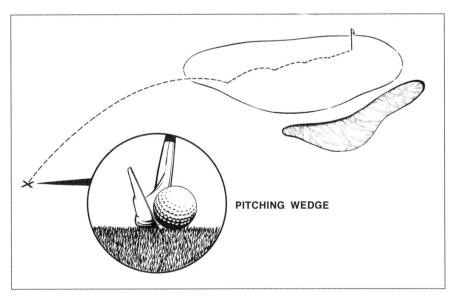

PITCHING WEDGE

The pitch-and-run is the ideal shot to hit when an open entranceway to the green allows you to feed the ball to the hole.

should automatically be ahead of the ball so that the clubface is hooded—that is, it's carrying a little less loft than normal.

3. *Clubface square to target.* In executing the pitch-and-run, the action will be dominated by your arm and shoulder swing, while the lower body remains relatively still. Swing the club back with your wrists firmer than for a normal pitch. The amount of your weight shift will vary with the length of the shot (and of your arm swing), but generally you'll have much less lower body weight shift on the pitch-and-run. Make sure to keep your right knee braced and your head still, directly over the ball.

Practice in various situations to determine the length of swing needed for the shot at hand. Generally, it will reach no more than a three-quarter position, with the clubshaft halfway between pointing to the sky and parallel to the ground.

On the downswing, again, pull the club down in a fairly steep arc with your left arm and hand controlling the action. Since you've shifted little weight to the right on the backswing, there will be little body movement toward the target on the downswing. You'll contact the ball before the clubhead's lowest point.

One adjustment you'll need to make for the pitch-and-run is in the follow-through. Whenever you want to keep the ball low, remember to keep the follow-through *low.* Finish with your arms extended and the clubshaft pointing at your target.

This type of action will produce a low-flying pitch that will carry some backspin. However, because you're playing the shot to firm ground, the shot will take several skidding bounces, then release a little more after the last full bounce.

Hard, honest practice is required to get the feel for the various amounts of carry and roll you'll produce with different clubs and on different ground conditions. It's the smart player who has the pitch-and-run in his or her bag to fall back on—particularly in windy conditions or in late summer, when many courses have dried out.

COUPLES'S CLINIC

15 LOWDOWN ON LIES

Handicap players can take a great cue from the pros by becoming more aware of how the lie of the ball can affect their shorter approach shots. This is an often-overlooked factor.

You probably know that virtually all Tour pros have the holes they play marked off, so they always know the exact yardage to the pin. They not only know the yardage but also understand how the lie of the ball might affect the shot. Say, for example, I know I've got eighty-eight yards to the pin. If I've got a nice clean fairway lie, I'll plan to play the shot to carry nearly the full eighty-eight yards and stop quickly upon landing.

However, say the shot is stopped in a bit of fluffy fairway grass or in some light rough. Pros know that this innocent-looking shot may jump a little off the face of the wedge, so that it carries less backspin and will run more after landing. So assuming there is enough green to work with, I may decide to play the shot as if it were eighty or eighty-two yards, rather than the actual eighty-eight.

On the other side of the coin, top players know from experience that on an eighty-eight yard pitch from a lie in deep rough the heavy grass will almost certainly have a "muffling" effect on impact. So they might play the shot as if it were one hundred yards long, not eighty-eight.

The moral: know not only the distances on your short shots but the effect of the particular lie on the shot's actual carry and roll. It's a key factor in hitting your short shots stiff to the hole.

16 THE ULTIMATE SWING GOVERNOR

While you should keep both feet slightly turned out when you're trying to obtain maximum distance, I believe you should set your right foot nearly square to the target line on your short swings. That's because the squared-up right toe acts as a control factor or governor on the length of your backswing.

Try this yourself. Stand at address in front of a full-length mirror. Angle your right foot out as you would for a full drive. Now make your backswing turn. Look in the mirror. Do you see how fully both your shoulders and hips have coiled?

Next, assume your address position with your right foot perpendicular to the target line. Again, make your backswing turn. This time, your shoulder turn will be slightly less and your hip turn will be substantially less. When you're making a short-iron or pitch swing, this right foot swing governor works in your favor, because the emphasis is on eliminating lateral movement and staying still over the ball while striking a downward blow. So remember to turn in that right foot whenever you're in pitching range.

17 BACK IT UP!

There's not much difference between the actual swings for your long, or power, swing and your short-shot swing. Except for a few swing modifications, most of the difference is controlled by the alterations in your setup.

The main setup difference is in your ball position at address. Instead of playing the ball forward, position it opposite the center of your stance. This accomplishes two things. First, you're assured that you'll make contact while the club is still on its descent instead of when it's at the very bottom of its arc. This means that if your lie is less than ideal, you're more likely to catch the ball first while getting as little grass as possible between club and ball. Thus you're less likely to hit a flier, which sails farther in the air and carries less spin on landing. Second, playing the ball farther back, with the inherent steeper angle of attack, will put more backspin—and more control—on your shots.

18 GET A GRIP

In Chapter 2, I suggested that the majority of amateurs would benefit from taking on a somewhat stronger grip position. This means that for a right-handed player, both hands should be turned relatively more to the right on the club handle than many teachers have recommended. This positioning is particularly helpful to those who slice their long shots.

There will be occasions on the shorter shots, however, when an adjustment to a relatively weaker position may help you hit the ball close to the hole. Say, for example, that you face a short-iron shot from the right side of the fairway, to a pin tucked on the front-right of the green, behind a bunker. If you play the shot with your normal grip and swing, you'll have to play the shot perfectly to get it close. If you draw the shot at all, you'll have to settle for the middle of the green, at best.

If you need to land the ball close to the cup in this situation, you must hit an extrasoft shot that *fades* toward the pin from left to right. To accomplish this, align the leading edge of your iron square to the flagstick. Then assemble your grip with both hands turned slightly more to the left on the handle. Your checkpoints for this adjusted hand position are that your left thumb should be positioned on the top center of the grip (rather than the top right) and, as you look down at your left hand, you should see only one (rather than two) knuckles.

This grip tends to return the clubface through the ball in a slightly open position relative to the swing path. Thus the shot will fly a little high and soft, with a touch of fade. It will also kick a bit to the right on landing, which helps you whenever the pin is tucked right.

Practice with this adjusted grip for the extrasoft short iron shot. Finally, remember to align your body slightly left of the target, because the shot will fade. Also remember that the soft, faded shot will fly a little higher and shorter than normal. To compensate, you'll probably want to play a less-lofted club.

19 TAKE A STRONG HOLD

Sometimes you'll run into a pitching situation in which the pin is placed on the top tier of a multilevel green. If there's trouble behind the green, it's risky to try to fly the ball all the way back and stop it. A wiser approach is to hit a lower approach that lands just below the top tier and skips up to the pin.

One way to hit the lower short iron is to adjust your grip just the opposite of the way you would for the high shot. That is, strengthen your grip, by turning both hands more to the right on the handle. As a checkpoint, the *V* formed by the thumb and forefinger of each hand should point up at your right shoulder, as you stand at address.

In playing this shot, align the clubface square to your target and set up slightly to the right of the target. Select the club that will land the ball on the level below the pin, and make your normal short-iron swing.

Your shot should start out a shade right of your target, in a slightly lower-than-normal trajectory, then draw slightly toward the flag. If struck properly, the ball will take two long skips, enough to climb to the top tier, then settle quickly.

Remember that by strengthening your grip and hitting a low, drawing short iron, you'll get a little more distance than you normally would. So factor this in to your club selection.

20 BETWIXT AND BETWEEN

Often, after you assess your yardage and lie for a short-iron shot, you'll conclude you're exactly halfway between two clubs. For example, you're 130 yards from the flag, the lie is good, and you hit your normal, controlled nine-iron 125 yards, your normal eight-iron 135 yards. What do you do?

In general, I recommend that when you're between clubs you should almost always go with the *longer* of the two clubs—in this case, the eight-iron. As I've stated earlier, you should never feel you have to hit a short iron as hard as you can to reach the pin. Sure, you probably can hit a nine-iron 130 yards (or whatever the between-club situation is). But my question is this: how likely arc you to hit it perfectly straight and perfectly solid, while reaching back for something extra? The only time I recommend this strategy is on an open driving hole where you'll benefit from extra yardage off the tee.

It's much easier to take the longer club and make a nice, controlled swing that's just a little more compact than normal. The chances are good that you'll maintain your best balance and rhythm throughout the stroke, make pure contact, and drop the ball safely onto the green and, we hope, close!

21 DON'T BE "GONE WITH THE WIND"

When average golfers find themselves in a short-iron situation, with a strong wind at their back, they usually take two clubs or so less than normal, then loft a high shot that's carried by the wind and rolls quite a bit after landing. Such a high-ball strategy is fine for a tee shot, but when your goal is to hit the ball close to the hole, it may not be the best.

During the 1991 Ryder Cup matches, I learned a lot from my veteran foursomes and fourball partner, Ray Floyd. In the predominantly windy seaside conditions, I noticed that on pitches for which there was an opening to the pin, Ray would hit a relatively low, semipunch shot, even straight downwind. Instead of hitting a high, hard-pitching wedge, for example, Ray would play a controlled nine-iron, using a three-quarter swing and hitting down and through the shot crisply. Floyd's rationale is that the lower you can keep the ball, even downwind, the more control you have over the distance it flies. You also put a little more backspin on the shot with this technique, so it's easier to predict how far the ball will skip on the green after it lands.

After watching Ray play these short, downwind approaches so masterfully all week, I realized it was an approach that would help me get these tricky shots to finish closer. I think it will do the same for you.

22 THE BALL GAME

Here's some equipment advice, directed particularly to the readers whose home courses leave them with a lot of shortish approach shots to small greens.

If your score depends largely on hitting soft, quick-stopping shots into the greens, you'd be wise to consider playing a balata-covered ball. The reason is that balata is still the softest cover material available, despite the vast improvement in many of the synthetics used. Since balata is inherently softer, the clubface grips it more readily, giving it a higher backspin rate than most synthetics do. This is a helpful characteristic not only on short-iron shots but also on many green-side chips, pitches, and bunker shots.

A really hard ball is likely to give you more total distance off the tee and might resist hook or slice spin a little more than a balata ball. But the gains as you approach the flag will probably be greater with balata.

4 | THE GREEN-SIDE GAME

How to Chip and Play Sand Shots Like a Pro

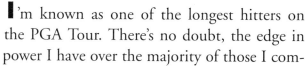

I'm known as one of the longest hitters on the PGA Tour. There's no doubt, the edge in power I have over the majority of those I compete against has a lot to do with the success I've achieved in recent years. But believe me, length and accuracy in the long swing are not the only reasons for that success. I've developed the ability to play the variety of chips, short pitches, and sand shots that comprise "the short game," with a high degree of sensitivity, imagination, and skill. These shots have proven every bit as valuable to me as my ability to drive the ball and hit the long irons powerfully and accurately. Improving this area of the game may be even more valuable to you.

Let me give you some statistics that will prove just how valuable an improved short game has been to me.

Nowadays, the PGA Tour staff is able to keep such detailed records that they even break down how many birdies you made on the par-three, -four, and -five holes; your birdie percentage on each of these types of holes; and your ranking on each. In 1992, I ranked first on the Tour in birdies on the par fives with a 47.6 birdie percentage. Granted, part of the reason I led this category is my overall length. But, any Tour player will tell you that a player who birdies a lot of par fives has to have a very well developed short game as well. Let me explain why.

On the PGA Tour, even I don't see many par fives that are easily reachable in two shots. Yes, there are quite a few par fives that I can reach in two if the wind and weather conditions are favorable and I hit two great shots. For example, at Augusta National, site of the Masters, I can reach all four par fives in two shots under normal conditions, although the two front-nine par fives—the second and eighth holes—are tougher to reach than Augusta's showcase back-nine par fives— the thirteenth and fifteenth holes.

We play a high percentage of very long par fives on the Tour. So I don't actually hit the putting surface of the par-five holes I play in two strokes all of the time. Yet I led the Tour in birdie percentage on these holes. It's obvious that to do that, my short game had to be as good as or better than that of other Tour players. I made many birdies by finessing the ball close to the hole with a good chip or pitch, after missing a par-five green with a long second shot or after purposely laying up. The short game is a vital weapon in my aggressive attack on the par-five holes.

Of course, the green-side game is even more important for most players as a key defensive element. You can save a hard-earned par after getting in trouble off the tee or missing the green with your approach shot. Think about this for a minute. During 1991 and 1992, I was the Vardon Trophy winner and led the PGA Tour in scoring average, at 69.59 and 69.38 strokes per round, respectively. Most of the courses we play have a par of 72, although some are par

71 or 70. So, it's fair to say I averaged approximately two strokes under par per round for those two years. Yet, in 1991, I hit 69.6 percent of the greens in regulation, and in 1992, I hit 71.4 percent. This means that over a two-year period I hit 12.6 greens in regulation figures or better and missed 5.4 greens per round, yet I averaged two under par for those rounds. The reason: I got the ball up and down quite a bit.

I take a lot of pride in my work around the greens. Certainly, you should too.

WHAT THE GREEN-SIDE GAME MEANS TO YOU

For the average amateur, the green-side game, if anything, contributes even more to the scores you post than to the Tour player. That's because you're almost sure to miss a lot more greens than the pros do. Whereas we might make all but six greens in an average round, you may be able to hit only a few, if any.

The instruction I've given you thus far will help you hit more greens in regulation. Still, on the majority of holes, you're going to have to get the ball "up and down" to make par. So the first thing I'm going to ask you to do is to start thinking about your green-side game the way a pro does. To me that kind of thinking can be capsulized into two phrases.

1. *Complete concentration.* We'll talk in specific detail about a variety of green-side situations and how to develop your ability to visualize and then execute the most effective recovery for each. But in general, I want you to commit yourself to giving every green-side shot your best concentration, creativity, and effort. This applies not only to your visualization of the kind of stroke you want to make but also to the lie of the ball, the condition and slope of the putting surface, and all other factors that influence the final result. You can't afford to play a green-side shot indifferently. You can't afford to be thinking of an earlier bad shot that caused you to be scrambling now. Learn to put all your focus on what you need to do to get it close and make that save.

I know this might sound like strange advice coming from me, because people sometimes perceive me as being so laid-back that I play all my shots casually, at less than 100 percent. I really don't think that's true. Looks can be deceiving. All I can say is that I know what my mind is focused on as I play each shot. If anything, I'm more focused on the green-side shots, because the individuality of each situation demands my complete attention.

2. *Always stay positive.* You'll become a much better green-side player if you teach yourself to stay in a positive mental framework in all short-game situations. Experience will help you realize that the majority of the shots you face aren't all that tough. In fact, on the more straightforward chips, you should often think in terms of *holing* the shot, not just getting it close.

During the 1991 Ryder Cup matches played on the Ocean Course at Kiawah Island, South Carolina, the U.S. team had its hands full in trying to wrest the Cup back from the Europeans. Late on the first day of play, my partner, Ray Floyd, and I were struggling to bring home a point in our four-ball match. At the fifteenth, a par four, my ball was short and left of the green in a tight lie, and I needed to pitch the ball over a corner of a trap to get to the pin, perhaps sixty feet away. It was definitely not an easy shot, but I remember being calm, focused, and positive in playing that stroke. With my *L*-wedge, I nipped the ball so that it comfortably carried the bunker and fringe, then ran neatly into the hole for a shocking birdie. The shot helped us hold on to our match and earn a sorely needed point. And we eventually won the Ryder Cup by the margin of a missed six-footer on the last hole of the tournament.

Now that I've provided you with some incentive to improve, let me show you my approach to the basic component of the short game: chipping.

A NEW LOOK AT CHIPPING

Many proficient short game players will tell you the best way to play your chip shots is relatively low and running, using a fairly

The standard way to chip is to land the ball on the fringe (left), then let it roll to the hole like a putt (right). Thanks to teacher Paul Marchand, I now use this method of chipping when it's better to feed the ball to the hole.

straight-faced iron. As the accompanying photographs show, the idea is to carry the ball in the air just far enough so it lands on the green, then rolls the rest of the way to the hole as smoothly as a putt.

For many years, I had difficulty visualizing and executing that type of low, running chip shot. Also, my loose-armed sweeping swing action that I do so naturally is not the best for this valuable shot that requires a very abrupt descending strike. But with the help of teacher Paul Marchand, I've worked real hard on this shot and have pretty much mastered it. I use it when it's better to feed the ball to the hole. It is actually a very reliable shot. I play the ball back in my stance, with my hands ahead of it. I set 60 to 70 percent of my weight on my left foot, and leave it there throughout the action to ensure a sharp descending hit at impact. I just make a small shoulder turn and drop the club on the ball. This is a handy shot; however, I also often prefer to hit *lofted* chip shots that land somewhat farther onto the green, then roll the shorter remaining distance to the hole.

Here's an analogy that might better help you see the difference between the two styles. The running chip can be likened to the action of a bowler in releasing the bowling ball down the lane. After he or she releases the ball from the hand, it's in the air for just a short distance before contacting the lane and rolling the rest of the way to the target.

In contrast, I like to imagine playing most chip shots more softly through the air. A useful image is to think of lobbing a softball toward a four-year-old child from, say, ten feet away. You want to make it as easy as possible for the child to catch the ball, so you toss it at a fairly high angle to give the child time to react. Of course, you don't want to throw a high pop-up that the child would have to gauge like a shortstop—you want to throw a nice, soft, lofted toss.

I'll get to the execution of this kind of chip stroke shortly. But first, let me explain why I think it's so useful, particularly on modern-day golf courses.

Many of today's courses feature greens that are more severely mounded and sloped than might have been the case twenty years ago. Say you have a chip shot that will cover sixty feet of green. If you plan to land the ball just onto the putting surface, you may have to read two or three different breaks perfectly to chip it close to the hole.

However, say you decide to play more of a lob-style chip, so you carry the ball thirty feet onto the green and let it roll the other thirty feet. In this case, you only need to read the green between the point at which the ball will land and the hole. Thus you reduce the number of calculations you need to make and simplify your shot-planning process.

In general, I hit these chips with the higher-lofted clubs: nine-iron, pitching wedge, sand wedge, and *L*-wedge. Work with these

I often prefer to hit lofted chip shots that fly most of the way to the hole.

clubs from various positions around the green, getting accustomed to the carry and roll each provides. Relying on only four clubs will simplify your club selection process.

Now that you know the difference between these strokes, let's discuss the mechanics of the lofted chip.

A MINIATURIZED NATURAL STROKE

I try to play this chip shot basically the same way I swing the club on my full shots. I recommend that you do the same. The time-honored advice regarding the chipping stroke is that it be a relatively brief, firm-wristed, punching action, in which you assume an address position with your hands well ahead of the ball, your weight mostly on your left foot, and the ball positioned back in your stance. All these address adjustments promote a steep descending motion in which the club strikes the ball in a de-lofted position, so the ball stays low to the ground. As I said earlier, there are certain situations in which a firm-wristed, hands-leading approach is desirable, even necessary. But I don't believe it's the best approach all of the time.

Instead, consider adopting my more natural method, considering the following points.

1. *Weight evenly balanced.* For most chip shots, my weight is divided evenly between the feet.

2. *Ball positioned just ahead of center.* Assuming you have a reasonably good lie, try playing the ball at the center or just ahead of center in a fairly narrow stance. It's a good idea on short chips to keep your stance (and your body) slightly open in relation to your target. This will help you see the target more clearly as you're settling in over the shot.

3. *Hands even with the ball.* Instead of assuming your address with your hands well ahead of the ball, try moving them back to level with the ball, as I suggested for the iron shot. This will help you hit the ball cleanly, just at the bottom of your stroke. You can put the whole clubface on the ball this way. Hitting the ball with the center of the clubface provides you with a much better feel and better control of your distance.

4. *Right hand controls the backswing.* Start your backswing by taking the club back smoothly from the ball, using your right hand and employing a small shoulder turn to control the movement. At the top of the backswing, let your right wrist hinge slightly rather than trying to make a stiff-wristed stroke. I think you'll find that these backswing actions further enhance your feel.

You'll notice that by using a touch of wrist action in your lofted chipping stroke, the clubhead will move in a *U*-shaped arc, rising well off the ground at the top of the backswing. Don't try to keep the clubhead unnaturally low by keeping your wrists ultrastiff. I think this sometimes produces a wooden-type stroke that reduces the clubhead feel you'll get by letting the right wrist hinge naturally.

The longer the chip, the higher the clubhead will rise off the ground. With practice, you'll get the feel for exactly how you'll carry the ball with varying clubs and varying lengths of backstroke. There's really no substitute for developing this awareness and feel for distance. In the long run, this will be practice time well spent, as you'll develop the ability to control closely the total distance—the combined carry and roll—you hit your chips. And distance control is the most important factor in chipping. You're much more likely to run a chip shot ten feet past the hole or leave one ten feet short than you are to hit one ten feet off-line.

5. *Release the club freely through the ball.* You should feel you're releasing the club freely on the downswing with your right hand and wrists, so the clubhead describes the same *U*-shaped arc as it did going back. As you make contact, the clubhead will be moving on the rather shallow path I advocate, rather than chopping down sharply.

As in the full swing, I don't mechanically force my left hand to lead the clubhead past impact. I think this is a needlessly unnatural move. Trust your natural hand release to square the clubface to your target at impact, and you'll achieve a soft, controlled flight that is the basis for improved chipping results. It's a small swing.

As I noted earlier, my lofted chipping method does require some practice. The stroke should not be difficult to master, because it's so natural. In fact, the only thing you have to do is to understand and practice the difference between the firm-wristed method and the lofted method. However, you'll need to adjust your entire visualization of the shot so that you learn to pick the proper landing spot (closer to the hole) required by your more lofted club and lob-style stroke to roll the ball stiff to (or in!) the cup.

AN EASY TRANSITION INTO PITCHING SITUATIONS

When does a chip shot become a green-side pitch shot? There's no set definition, because really, one shot gradually flows into the other. If you miss a green by, say, five yards or less and there's nothing but fringe grass between your ball and the green, you have a straightforward chip shot. If your ball is twenty yards off the putting surface with open ground between it and the green, the question is whether you have to execute a pitch shot or a chip shot. You could reasonably call for a chip, particularly if there's plenty of green to work with in front of the cup. On the other hand, if your ball is off the green by twenty yards with a bunker, a steep slope, or deep rough between it and the green, there's really no choice but to hit a high-lofted wedge shot, which will carry the trouble and stop the ball quickly near the hole. Here, you've definitely got a green-side pitch.

My point in trying to differentiate between a lofted chip shot and a pitch is that there really is very little distinction between them. And you'll find that you execute the short game best if you don't make any clear distinction between the mechanics used for lofted chipping and for green-side pitch shots. *The green-side pitch is simply a longer version of your lofted chip stroke, played with a more lofted club.*

The relaxed and natural chipping setup and stroke action that you have developed will help you when the shot is extended to a short pitch. You simply need to lengthen your lofted chipping action, adding to the length and force of swing as necessary to carry the ball the longer distance.

Because of the basic requirements of the shot, you'll always be playing a green-side pitch with one of the wedges: the pitching wedge, the sand wedge, or if you carry it as I do, an extralofted or *L*-wedge. Experiment with the three pitching clubs to learn just which club will stop the ball near the flag from any position around the green. Although every player is different, I'd guess that most amateurs would benefit from having a third wedge in their bag. That's because they generally miss more greens than they hit, and they likely face several of these shots per round. Thus amateur golfers will get more use out of a lofted wedge than they will from one of the long irons.

With these thoughts in mind, let's go through the planning, setup, and swing processes that apply to various green-side pitching situations.

The Basic Green-side Pitch

I refer to the "basic" green-side pitch as any shot of twenty or more yards that must carry over bunkers, mounds, or rough when the ball is lying reasonably well in the fairway or light rough and you have more than enough green to work with to stop the ball near the hole.

For the basic pitch I'll almost always use the sand wedge. As with the lofted chip, I suggest you play the ball slightly ahead of center in a narrow, open stance. Distribute your weight pretty much evenly between the feet or, if anything, place a touch more weight on your right side at address. When the lie is good, your hands should be even with the ball or behind it slightly. Assuming you have a cushioned lie, this hand position will encourage you to deliver the clubhead to the ball with its full loft (usually about fifty-five degrees), for the high, soft trajectory you want.

If you have enough green to work with, your clubface should be just a little open to your target. I like to put a touch of cutting action on all my green-side pitches, and I think you'll find your control will be enhanced if you do so too. So keep the clubface open just a little.

As with the chip stroke, your right hand and shoulder turn should control the take-away and backswing action. The clubhead will describe a *U*-shaped arc on both the backswing and through swing. Let your right wrist and right elbow hinge naturally as you approach the top of the backswing. This will add rhythm and fluidity to the stroke, which you just won't attain with the firm-wristed style. Your downswing should feature the same free right hand and wrist release through the ball, so that the clubhead

A relaxed finish indicates that you executed the basic green-side pitch correctly.

slides through the grass at a fairly shallow angle, then comes up quickly after impact with a ladling action.

This shallow-bottomed, somewhat wristy style, combined with an open-faced action, produces a high shot that stops fairly quickly. If you execute the shot as described, you'll find you can usually carry the ball most of the way to the hole. For example, say you're twenty-five yards from the flag and pitching to a medium speed, fairly flat green. Using this technique, you'd want to land the ball between ten to fifteen feet short of the hole. Of course, if the green is fast and/or running away from you, you'll need to land the ball farther from the hole; if the putting surface is extraslow, you'll find you can loft the ball to just a few feet short of the hole and it will stop almost dead.

The Super-lob

The super-lob is an extension of the basic green-side pitch, but it flies even higher and stops even more quickly. It is particularly useful when the conditions are similar to those for the basic green-side pitch, except that the pin is tucked close to the near side of the green or the green is fast and running away from you.

Here are the setup and swing adjustments that you need to make to the basic pitch shot to hit the super-lob:

1. Assuming the lie is good, place the ball more forward, opposite your left instep at address.
2. Your hands should be positioned slightly farther behind the ball.
3. You should place about two-thirds of your weight on your right foot at address.
4. Both your body and your clubface alignments should be slightly more open to the target line.
5. If you carry an *L*-wedge, this is definitely the time to use the sixty degrees or so of loft it offers.

The execution of this shot is an exagerrated version of the basic pitch. The right hand controls the stroke and adds even more hing-

When preparing to hit a super-lob shot, it's critical that the ball be played opposite the left instep.

ing motion to the top of the backswing and the follow-through. At this point, I make a slight alteration for the super-lob. Starting down, I "loop" the club slightly more inside on the downswing than for the basic pitch. If you get used to setting up well left with the clubface very open you can get this one to stop dead.

Always try to play this shot with a very slow, leisurely tempo so you meet the ball while using the full loft of the clubface. Strive to keep your head very still, because there is slightly more chance of mis-hitting this shot. Finally, remember that the super-lob will require even more length of swing than the basic green-side pitch, since you're hitting a shot that's even higher and softer.

The Down-lie Pitch

So far we've talked about situations in which the lie is reasonably good, so you can get the leading edge of your wedge under the ball. Unfortunately, you'll also run into situations in which the ball is sitting down snugly in rough. Here's how to handle them.

When the ball is down in grass, you'll need to hit down on the shot more instead of ladling it. Therefore, set up for that shot by:

- Playing the ball back a bit, so that it's opposite the center point of your narrow stance
- Placing your hands slightly ahead of the ball
- Putting slightly more weight on your left side

As for club selection, an *L*-wedge is ideal because it features greater loft than either the pitching wedge or sand wedge. Therefore, it can help you stop the ball fairly quickly, even from this tricky lie.

With your hands ahead at address, you may feel as if your backswing were a little quicker than that for the lob pitch, although you shouldn't consciously speed up the swing. Your downstroke will automatically be on a more descending plane because of your hands-ahead setup position. You'll hit the ball just before the bottom of your swing, instead of at the beginning of your upswing, since the ball was back a little farther at address. Because you'll strike down a bit more sharply, you'll also find that the impact with the rough grass serves to abbreviate the follow-through slightly.

The result of these changes is that the ball will leave the clubface at a lower angle than for the basic pitch or super-lob; that's the price you pay for making sure you make good contact with the ball from a

The down-lie pitch is the recovery shot to play when the ball is sitting down snugly in grass.

bad lie. So count on the ball landing at a shallower angle and running farther.

If the pin is either on the middle of the green or on the far side, you can probably land the ball on the green yet stop it at the hole. If the pin is tucked on your side, however, you might be wise to accept your medicine and expect to run the ball by the hole, take your two putts, and go to the next hole.

There are some occasions when the super-lob technique is a great choice for the down lie pitch. It takes practice, but the key is to allow for hitting the grass behind the ball, very similar to a sand shot. If executed correctly, the ball comes out very softly.

A final positive note on the down-lie pitch: if the ball is lying on hardpan, as opposed to down in the rough, you'll find you can put bite on the ball and make it stop quicker than you might think. Factor this quick-stopping action into your strategy.

The Up Lie

Sometimes you'll find yourself with a green-side pitch (or chip) for which the ball is perched on the top of some deep rough. This shot looks very inviting because you know you can get all of the clubface on the ball and loft it nicely. *Two words of caution:* be careful! Although it looks like a cinch shot, the "up" lie is a teaser. Basically, you have to make sure you don't slide the club completely through the cushion underneath the ball, so you just graze the underside of the ball and bloop it a few feet forward.

Here are some adjustments to make to the basic pitch shot that allow you to play a nice soft lob, while not undercutting the ball and coming up short:

1. *Choke down on the grip approximately one inch.* Because the ball is well above the surface of the ground, choking down shortens the club slightly so that you can use the same swinging motion and confidently expect clean contact.

2. *Square the clubface.* Instead of laying the clubface back for more loft, set it square so that there's more clubface directly behind the ball; this means less chance of the club sliding underneath.

3. *Set up with the bottom of the clubhead level with the bottom of the ball.* Grounding the club with this type of lie can cause the ball to sink into the grass, giving you a one-stroke penalty. And you must replace the ball, or it is a two-stroke penalty!

Other than these fine-tuning points, go ahead and play the shot using your basic green-side pitch setup and stroke method. Keep your head very still and you'll pop the ball nicely within one-putt range.

SAND PLAY: GET SLAPHAPPY

For most high handicappers, green-side sand shots are terrifying. Basically, I think the fear stems from the fact that they have only a vague idea of what they're trying to accomplish. They know they have to hit the ball out, but they also know that in most cases they're not supposed to contact the ball itself. Most of the time, my Pro-Am partners seem to end up swinging away in a panicky sort of funk, hoping they do something right and the ball pops out and onto the green—*anywhere* on the green is just fine, they'll take it.

To me this kind of thinking is negative. I believe the basic green-side sand shot is one of the easiest in golf. I know it sounds a little cocky to say that, but I believe it's true, and the PGA Tour's statistics back that up: in 1992, I got the ball up and down in two from green-side bunkers 57.8 percent of the time. That means whether I faced a short or long bunker shot, out of a perfect lie or a not-so-good one, I had to be laying the ball close to the cup pretty darn regularly.

There are two reasons why I've developed into a good bunker player, and they're not all that complex.

First, early in my career I obtained a good, clear understanding

Before you can be a good green-side sand player, you must realize the physics of the shot: you hit into the sand and under the ball so that the sand lifts the ball out of the bunker. You do not hit the ball.

of the actual physics of the sand shot: I realized that the sand lifts the ball and the standard sand shot gives you the greatest margin for error of any shot in golf. Knowing this really took the fear factor out of the shot.

Second, the fairly wristy-style stroke with a lazy looping action I usually employ when chipping and pitching is absolutely tailor-made for the green-side sand shot.

Now you're starting to understand why I'm so high on the idea of approaching virtually all your short game shots with the idea of making a natural, flowing, wristy swing action: it *integrates* your entire short game into a harmonious whole. Whether you land in a bunker, in some rough down a slope off the green, or on the fringe with a simple straightforward chip, your short game stroke will stay pretty much the same. So when you're practicing one short game shot, you'll also be practicing the others.

What are you trying to accomplish when your ball finds a green-side bunker? First, let's address those golfers whose goal is simply to get the ball onto the green consistently. For any normal sand shot, all you need to do is *splash a slice of sand out of the bunker—the slice that has the ball on top of it.* I recommend that you visualize, for every basic bunker shot, cutting out a fairly thin slice of sand, one that starts at a spot two inches behind the ball. This approach will give you a standardized picture of what you're trying to accomplish in the stroke and remove the confusion that you may have about the shot. You'll learn that you can control the length of the shot simply by varying the force of your swing.

Basic Bunker Shot Technique

For the normal green-side sand shot, from a reasonable lie, here are the basics to keep in mind in setting up the shot.

1. Wiggle your feet *lightly* into the sand. Work your spikes in just a little below the surface of the sand so you feel secure; you don't have to build a sand castle in there like you see some Sunday golfers do. In fact, if you dig in too deep, you'll actually get yourself below the level of the ball. This tends to make you hit the sand too far behind the ball, to hit it fat, and possibly to leave it in the bunker. So just get a secure stance in the sand.

2. Open the blade of your sand wedge. I should mention here that you must have a good sand wedge with a fairly generous bounce. This bounce acts as sort of a *rudder* and allows the clubhead to take a shallow cut rather than digging deeply into the sand.

3. Open the clubface at address, about the same number of degrees you align your body to the left. For example, for a short, pop sand shot, your clubface and stance should be very open, about twenty-five degrees each. However, on a medium-long sand shot, say seventy-five feet, both your clubface and stance should be just a touch open. This setup will encourage a swing that's more square to the target, automatically giving the ball more forward impetus and less sidespin.

4. Your weight should favor the *right* side. This setup is particularly helpful in playing the basic sand shot, because you want the clubhead to slice shallowly through the sand two inches behind the ball. If you're leaning toward the left, it's harder to accomplish this.

5. The ball and hands should be in the

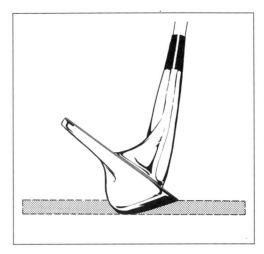

When choosing a sand wedge, pick one with a fairly generous bounce.

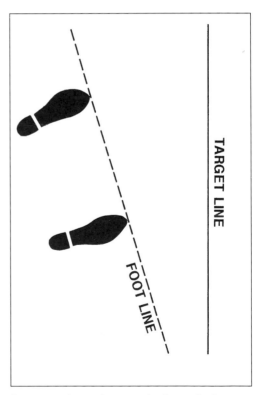

An open stance is a must when playing a basic bunker shot.

super-lob position. If the lie is good, position the ball opposite your left instep. As with the super-lob from grass, your hands should be a shade behind the ball.

6. Grip down just slightly on the club, say a half to three-quarters of an inch. By using virtually the whole length of the club, you'll retain the relatively heavy feel of the sand wedge throughout the swinging action. This will help you maintain a slow swing tempo, which is a key to proficient bunker play.

In executing the basic sand shot stroke, let your right hand and forearm be active. As you draw the club back, let your right wrist and elbow hinge immediately after the take-away is completed or just as your hands are moving past your right knee. As you continue to cock your right wrist, the clubhead will begin to describe a steep arc, one that's much narrower than for most fairway shots.

Your swing movement should be controlled mainly by your arms and shoulder turn. Any weight shift in the lower body should be minimal, simply a slight response to the backward and forward motion of your arms and the turning of your shoulders.

The ease in this shot is the lazy loop with the hands and arms to the inside on the downswing and the wrist and left arm recock on the follow-through that allows you to keep the clubface open all the way through the release.

As I mentioned earlier, you'll control the distance you carry the shot mainly by the length of backswing, while you focus on delivering the club's bounce to a spot two inches behind the ball. By learning to hit consistently that same spot, you'll quickly see that lofting the ball out of the bunker every time is easy. You just need to practice to determine how far back and through you must swing for a twenty-, forty-, or sixty-foot bunker shot and how to judge the amount of force needed for the type of sand—heavy or light—you're playing on.

After just a couple of practice sessions using this simple approach, you'll start instinctively to make the adjustments in swing force you need to meet the distance requirements of the shot at hand.

Let's get back to playing the stroke itself. Once you've reached the length of backswing you need, your right wrist should have cocked pretty substantially—the fuller the swing, the greater the wrist hinge. Remember to keep your tempo smooth, particularly as you make the transition from backswing to downswing.

As you start down, keeping your focus firmly on that spot two inches behind the ball, you should immediately begin uncocking that right wrist hinge. Imagine

To improve your bunker play, plan to deliver the club into a spot two inches behind the ball.

your entire downswing as a kind of slapping motion controlled by your right hand. Your aim is to slap the sand smartly two inches behind the ball, so you slice a fairly shallow cut of sand, about six inches long, up and out of the bunker. The golf ball will automatically pop up and out with the sand.

Your follow-through will be somewhat abbreviated compared with a full fairway shot, because you'll meet more resistance in slapping the sand and because you've taken less than a full swing to begin with. Still, make sure that you keep the club moving through and beyond impact. Many high handicappers have a tendency to chop at the ball, leaving the clubhead—and the ball—in the sand. Keep the clubhead moving up in a U-shaped arc into the follow-through, with about as much follow-through as backswing for the given length of shot.

Results of the Slaphappy Technique—And a Secret Benefit

Given this execution from a reasonable lie, the result will be a shot that gets up in the air quickly and lands softly, so you can stop the ball near any pin position. The shot should also be carrying a fair amount of backspin and also a trace of cut spin, owing to the glanc-

To extract the ball safely out of sand, accelerate the club through impact.

ing blow of having the clubface open and your body aligned left.

Practice will tell you just how far you are able to carry the ball to the flag. In general, if the lie is very clean, you can plan on flying the ball almost all the way to the hole. If it's down a touch, the ball will come out a bit lower, so play for a bit more bounce and run after it lands.

One of the great things about using the constant "two-inch-behind-the ball" approach is that it gives you a greater margin for error than on any other shot in golf. Why? Even if you miss your impact spot by, say, one-half inch in either direction, the end result of your shot stays pretty much the same. In effect, you have a total impact *range* of one inch (one-half inch behind your spot to one-half inch ahead of it) that will allow your ball to travel the same total distance.

Here's why it happens. Say you have a fifty-foot bunker shot. You make the necessary length swing but slap the sand two and one-half inches behind the ball—in effect, a little fat. Well, the ball will fly a little shorter than you intended, but because it won't have as much backspin, it will run a little more, so that the total distance is nearly the same. The slightly fat sand shot usually runs out to finish close to the hole.

Conversely, suppose you slap the sand only one and one-half inches behind the ball. You splash the shot out neatly with little sand to resist the club, so the ball flies a bit farther than you want—all the way to the hole on the fly. However, this slightly clean shot will be loaded with backspin, so after one small bounce, it stops dead or even sucks back to the hole. So you see, either way you have a margin of error on your point of impact for the normal sand shot. Knowing this will give you more confidence in your sand game.

The Two Biggest Challenges in Sand Play: The Buried Lie and the Long Bunker Shot

No discussion about sand play would be complete without covering situations other than the basic, middle-distance sand shot. Let's take a few minutes to understand the adjustments needed for two of the most common variations.

Buried-lie Play

Suppose your home course features bunkers with relatively soft, deep sand. You'll find that a fair percentage of your shots will plug, so that half or more of the ball lies beneath the sand's surface, which constitutes the "buried" lie.

For this shot, most of the adjustments are made to your setup. You'll need to attack the ball with a sharper downswing angle to get the leading edge under the ball. To help you accomplish this, you should move the ball back about four inches, to a point nearly opposite the center of your stance, and move your hands forward so they are ahead of the ball.

Your stance and the face of your wedge should be set square to the flag rather than open. Also, your weight should favor your left foot slightly instead of your right. As with the standard bunker

When playing from a buried lie in sand, set the clubface square to your target.

shot, aim to contact the sand two inches behind the ball.

In executing the shot, swing the club up on a steep arc dominated by your arms. The hands-ahead/ball-back setup will help you do this. Furthermore, because of this left-side-dominated setup position, you'll find that your right hand is more passive and will not cock the club as much at the top. That's okay. Keeping your head stock-still, firmly swing the club down into the sand behind the ball. Because of the steep entry, you'll have little or no follow-through. The ball will pop out of its buried position like a knuckleball, with no backspin. So plan on the ball running about twice as far as it carries. For example, if you're sixty feet from the hole, you may have to carry it just twenty feet and let it run the rest of the way. By the way, this shot usually pops out to the right of target, so aim a little left.

One additional note: when the ball is severely buried, simplify the shot by playing your pitching wedge instead of your sand wedge. With its sharp leading edge and modest bounce, the pitching wedge will cut into the sand instead of giving you the slapping action.

There will be times where you've drawn a buried lie and the pin is tucked close to where the ball rests, so you have little green to work with. My advice is to stick with the method I've just described and make sure you get the ball out (or try Ken Venturi's four-iron method). The smart play here is to work the percentages and land the ball somewhere on the green. Then take your two putts (maybe you'll even sink it!) and go the next tee, knowing that you've cut your losses. Sure, every now and then Chi Chi Rodriguez or Gary

Player or even I can pull off a remarkable finesse shot from a buried lie. But the odds are against the shot, even for us, so use your head and you'll come out ahead.

Solving the Dreaded Long Bunker Shot
Every now and then you'll find yourself in a bunker that's situated some fifteen to forty yards from the green's nearest edge. This leaves you in that precarious "long bunker shot" situation—one in which the total distance to the flag is from twenty-five to fifty yards. The problem is that you eventually reach a distance, which depends on your own strength, at which you can't get the ball all the way to the hole using the standard bunker shot technique. Thus it is important to learn adjustments that can lengthen your sand shot range. Let me explain them in steps that you can bring into play as the length of the shot increases.

1. *Know your full-length normal shot.* The first thing you must know is how far you can hit a sand shot with your normal technique, which includes a slightly open stance and clubface plus a full, yet controlled, swing. Practice your basic technique so you know what your cutoff length is.
2. *Square your stance and the clubface.* This adjustment makes the clubhead contact the sand while moving directly along the target line. It will also slap the sand with slightly less loft, so the ball comes out a bit lower and carries farther. This adjustment alone should do the trick when you're only several yards beyond your normal full sand shot distance.
3. *Slap the sand one inch closer to the ball.* When you need even more carry, say ten yards more than you can get by squaring your stance and the clubface, you have to take a bit more risk by reducing the amount of sand you take behind the ball. Make sure to keep your head very still, since you're forced into accepting a smaller margin for error on this shot.
4. *Use your pitching wedge.* If the length of shot is still out of your range, play the shot with a square-faced pitching wedge.

The pitching wedge normally carries five or six degrees less loft than the sand wedge, so this adjustment should add another eight to ten yards to your long bunker shot range.

You'll find that the adjustments offered in points two, three, and four will, when combined, roughly double your range from the sand. That is, if your normal, comfortable full bunker shot carries twenty-five yards, by incorporating all the points described, you should be able to increase your range to fifty yards. Of course, you need to practice to incorporate all these adjustments. The best way to ingrain them is by going out on the course in the evening with a half-dozen balls, when there's little play. Set up long bunker shots of varying distances. Learn each of the adjustments you need to increase your range the necessary amount.

In the introduction to this section, I made the case that sand play was easy. Let me conclude by saying that if you employ my techniques described here, I hope you'll learn to enjoy practicing your sand shots. Not only will that give you confidence in your sand play, but I know of no better practice to help reinforce the loose arm and wrist, rhythmical action that I advocate you use throughout your game.

COUPLES'S CLINIC

23 CHOOSE YOUR WEAPON

As mentioned, along with the traditional firm wrist chip, I recommend that you develop a relatively soft chipping style in which you lob the ball slightly farther in the air, with a little less run. The two advantages are that you'll have less green to read, and since you're playing a more lofted chip, you'll reduce the chance of confusion about club selection in chipping. Many golfers chip with as little loft as a five-iron. I suggest that unless you are just off the edge yet a long way from the hole, you should hit lofted chips with a maximum of four clubs: nine-iron, pitching wedge, sand wedge, and the third or *L*-wedge.

How far should you expect to carry and roll the ball with each of these chipping weapons? These vary, depending on whether you're chipping uphill or downhill and if the green speed is slow or fast. Given a fairly flat surface with medium speed (say, a reading of between seven and eight on a Stimpmeter), you should plan for the following carry-to-roll ratios:

Chipping Club	Percent Carry	Percent Roll
Nine-iron	50	50
Pitching wedge	60	40
Sand wedge	70	30
L-wedge	80	20

24 PRACTICE MAKES PERFECT

In setting up to play a chip shot, analyze all the factors that go into the shot—the lie; the distance to the hole; the slope, speed, and grain of the green from where your ball will land to the cup; and finally, the correct club for the shot. Once you've processed that information, assume your chipping address and execute a practice swing that's mechanically identical to the swing you think you'll need to employ when playing the actual shot. Next, set up to the ball and simply reproduce your "perfect" practice stroke.

Note: sometimes, as you make your practice stroke, something won't feel quite right. You may sense that the shot will require a little more or less force. If so, take the time to get the technique right. That way, you'll play your real chip with a high degree of confidence.

25 BULL'S-EYE

I've suggested an alternative chipping approach in which you lob the ball a longer distance toward the hole in the air. While this method has proved successful for me, you might need some help in adjusting if you're used to landing the ball just on the green and letting it race the rest of the way to the hole.

Here's an image that should help you. As you analyze the shot, imagine an archery target lying flat on the green, covering the area where you think the ball should land to roll the rest of the way to the cup. Then try to loft your chip so it lands right on the bull's-eye of the target.

This imagery helps in multiple ways. First, it will show you how accurately you're carrying the ball in relation to your desired landing spot. Are you consistently long or short? Or are you missing your target to either side? Observing where the ball is landing will clearly define any adjustments you need to make in the force or direction of your stroke. Soon you should be landing the ball on or very close to your own bull's-eye spot.

Second, using the bull's-eye will show you exactly what the outcome of the shot was when you carried the ball right where you planned. Did your chip shot go in the hole? If not, why not? Did it pull up short, slide six feet past, or bounce in a direction you didn't expect? If any of these occurred, the bull's-eye approach lets you know that your execution was perfect but your *judgment* was not. You may need to move your bull's-eye slightly closer to or back from the hole or to adjust its line slightly.

During chipping practice, play every chip to a bull's-eye, constantly adjusting your stroke until you land on target. Then, if you don't hole out, adjust your bull's-eye until hitting it also means your chip goes in the hole.

With bull's-eye practice, you'll be amazed at how many times you hole out from off the green in actual play.

26 NO HEAVY LIFTING

An awful lot of amateurs mis-hit simple chip shots time after time, usually skulling the shot so it scampers way past the cup. They often toss off this miscue by saying, "I lifted my head again." And they never understand the true basis of these missed shots. What really happens is that the typical player straightens his or her knees on the downswing, raising the head, hands, and club slightly.

If you lift and hit hard running chips past the hole, increase your knee flex and keep it constant throughout the stroke.

27 SAND CHEATERS

There will be times when you find your ball lying cleanly in a shallow green-side sand bunker that features little or no lip. If these circumstances are in your favor, take advantage of them. Play a chip or, preferably, even a putt.

Since even a good lie in sand is somewhat tight, assume the chipping address position you'd use for a tight lie from grass: hands ahead of the ball (which is positioned near the center of a narrow stance) and weight slightly favoring the left side. Make an arms-controlled stroke, while keeping your head dead still. If anything, try to hit this chip a shade thin rather than fat.

If there's no lip at all, you can use the putter. Gauge the total distance to the flag, then simply play it like a long putt, adding in a force factor for the sand and grass the ball must run through before reaching the green.

Practice these "sand cheaters" in advance. You never know when they'll come in handy.

28 DO THE BUMP

Too often you'll hit a good-looking approach that doesn't quite hold the green, trickling just off its edge, against the first cut of rough. You may not be far from the cup, but you have a tricky play. It's hard to control a chip, because the longer grass will get between your club and ball, making it hard to stop the shot. You could putt, but again the grass is likely either to catch the clubhead on the way back or to snuff the impact.

The safest shot in this situation is one that many pros—but few amateurs—turn to. It's the "bump" shot, played with the sand wedge. It's simple—you stroke the ball just as you would a putt, except that you use the leading edge of the sand wedge to contact the ball at its equator—just above the level of the grass behind the ball.

Hold the club up off the ground rather than down in the grass, so its leading edge lines up with the ball's equator. Use your normal putting grip and setup. Then, simply execute your normal stroke. Make sure to keep your head still by trying to watch that leading edge bump the ball. The ball will skid for a slight distance before picking up true overspin just as a putt would.

29 FLAG IN OR OUT?

Often you'll see a Tour pro have the flag pulled out for a short chip shot. It's interesting, because when this happens you know the player is thinking specifically of holing the shot. I believe, however, that you generally have a better chance of holing a chip if you leave the flag *in*.

The argument by those who pull the flag is that with it out, a chip with perfect line can't possibly hit the flag and ricochet out. Also, many players believe when they pull the flag, it makes them feel more confident that they'll make it.

I think that leaving the flag in will help you more than it can hurt you. Keep in mind that for the ball to drop into the hole when the flag is out, its speed has to be just about right. If it's running fast enough to go even a couple of feet past, it won't drop unless it hits the hole dead center.

The big advantage of leaving the flag in comes when you've hit the chip much too hard. Here, the flag helps you because there's no way the ball can drop otherwise. If you hit the flag, the ball may drop or at least bang the flag and stop within "gimme" range, rather than running well past the hole.

The only time to pull the flag is if it's leaning noticeably toward you, so the ball might not fit into the hole if it's struck perfectly. Other than that unusual circumstance, play the odds and leave the flag in.

30 DOWN AND DIRTY

Sometimes you'll find yourself with a green-side pitch or chip from a lie that makes it difficult to recover using your normal technique.

In such circumstances, move the ball back about two inches in your narrow, open stance. Move your hands two inches forward so they're ahead of the ball. Keep your weight mainly on your left side and concentrate on a still head. Make your normal firm-wristed chipping stroke. Your adjustments will cause you to strike the ball at the more descending angle necessary to ensure clean contact from a down lie.

Remember: this chip will fly lower and run a little farther than a lie that's sitting up. So in planning your shot, either move your bull's-eye—the spot where you want the ball to land—a little closer toward you or select a more lofted club to carry the ball to your ordinary bull's-eye position.

31 DON'T DIG

In a bunker, club golfers often look like they're doing the Watusi as they wiggle their feet back and forth, deep into the sand. When you overdo this, you make the sand shot more difficult than it needs to be.

In setting up, wiggle your feet in only to the depth at which you're sure your spikes won't slip during the swing. Generally, this will be about one-half inch below the sand's surface. When you work your feet way down into the sand, you've made the shot harder because, in effect, you've given yourself a sidehill lie with the ball above your feet. The tendency will be to contact the sand behind your target point. The result is that you leave the ball in the bunker or you hit it way short of the hole.

Dig in only as far as you need to. Also, choke up on the grip of your sand wedge a fraction of an inch to make up for the fact that digging in, even gently, puts you closer to the ball.

32 GO SLOW IN SAND

You've probably noticed that most amateurs make a quick, jabbing stroke on sand shots, rather than one with a slow, even tempo. It's almost as if they're hoping to get the shot over with quickly.

It's important to learn to swing the club s-l-o-w-l-y on every sand shot. One reason is that the sand wedge is the heaviest club in the bag. Therefore it's the hardest to keep under control if you make a quick swing. Second, this will help you develop the uniform *U*-shaped bottom to the swing that allows you to slap out a slice of sand that takes the ball with it. The slowness also allows you enough time to make the necessary amount of shoulder rotation and wrist and arm cocking/recocking actions. The quicker you swing, the choppier your downswing plane will be, which increases the chances of stabbing the shot and leaving the ball in the sand.

If you're a Speedy Gonzalez in sand, start back slowly and keep the same tempo on the downswing as you did going back. You'll find the ball popping up out of the sand every time.

33 *X* MARKS THE SPOT

The simplest and most reliable approach to green-side bunker shots is to slap the club into the sand at one specific spot behind the ball every time. This spot should be two inches behind the ball. It's helpful to draw an imaginary *X* in the sand where you want the bounce of your wedge to make contact. Focus on hitting that *X* every time. You can alter the distance the ball flies from the sand simply by altering the length of your swing.

Marking your spot with an *X* gives you a uniform approach and will aid your confidence. You don't have to worry about taking a lot of sand on one shot, then chipping right behind the ball on the next, and maybe getting your signals crossed. It's much easier merely to adjust the force of your swing.

34 MIRROR, MIRROR

One of the more obvious problems I see with amateur golfers is that they fail to follow through on sand shots. Instead, they stick the club in the sand, and as a result, the ball usually stays in the bunker too. A good image that helps overcome this destructive chopping tendency is what I refer to as "mirror, mirror." What this means is that you should more or less make the length of your follow-through a mirror image of the length of your backswing.

Say you have a really short, pop sand shot with the flag no more than twenty-five feet away. You may have to take the club only halfway back to generate the correct amount of force. Follow through the same distance. For a fifty-foot sand shot, when you need, say, a three-quarter-length backswing to cover the distance to the flag, imagine taking a three-quarter-length follow-through as well.

This mirror imagery will help you instinctively improve your slapping action of the club through the sand. *Note:* the mirror image applies to all sand shots from reasonable lies. If the ball is severely buried, you'll be forced to make a steeper downward dig, and the follow-through will be curtailed.

35 SAND SAVVY

Tailor your control of the distance you hit your bunker shots by developing "sand savvy." Depending on the type of sand, the ball may come out a lot farther or shorter than you thought it would. Basically, these are the points to be aware of:

1. *Larger-grained sand means a longer-distance shot.* When the sand grains are relatively large, the ball will usually sit up better, because the bigger grains support the ball's weight. The more the ball is up, the easier it is to splash it out. So from good lies in large-grained sand, use a little less swing force than you think for the needed distance.

2. *Fine-grained sand means a muffled shot.* If you play out of very fine, powdery sand—the kind that doesn't pack well—the ball's impact force will often cause it to be buried to some degree. So you could be playing your sand shot from a less-than-favorable lie. This sand will also give a little more, allowing the sand wedge's bounce to go a little deeper. The clubhead won't move forward as freely, and the shot is somewhat muffled. So from fine sand, add a little extra force than you may think you'd need from a particular distance.

3. *Know your depth.* No matter what type of sand, remember that the deeper it is, the shorter the shot will come out; the shallower the sand, the more the ball will carry. If the sand is deep, it's impossible for the bounce to get to the sand's base; thus the bounce will go deeper into the sand, so the ball comes out softer. If the sand is shallow, the bounce is likely to hit bottom and bounce back up. This means there'll be less sand between club and ball, so the shot comes out much faster.

Be alert to the texture and depth of the sand, particularly when you're away from your home course, and your sand savvy will pay dividends.

36 ALL WET

You might think when you're playing from wet sand, you'll have to hit the shot with much more force. Actually, the opposite is usually true. When the sand is damp, it will pack more than normal; thus it provides more resistance to the clubhead's bounce, so that a smaller cushion of sand will get between club and ball. Because of the packed sand, you must hit a little closer to the ball than the normal two inches to keep the leading edge of the sand wedge from bouncing into the ball.

If anything, your shots from wet sand will fly a little farther than those from dry sand. On wet sand, use a little less swing force than you think you'll need for the distance. Finally, keep in mind that from damp, packed sand, you'll get more bite; the ball should take one big hop, then stop!

37 KING OF THE HILL

Uphill and downhill sand lies cause lots of uncertainty and missed shots. Most amateurs don't know what adjustments to make. But once you understand the principles and practice them, you can become the "king of the hill" in these specialty situations.

UPHILL LIES

The tendency from an uphill lie is to pop the ball up high, leaving it short of the flag. The reason is that when you hit your X two inches behind the ball, you're hitting a spot that's also below the ball. So you'll get much more under the ball than from level sand, and you'll meet much more resistance.

Make sure to set your body *perpendicular* to the upslope at address, so your club will slap the sand at the same relative angle it would from a level lie.

Practice some shots and you might find this is all the correction you need. If you're still coming up short, you may also need to move your X slightly closer to the ball, say, one and one-half inches rather than two inches behind it.

DOWNHILL LIES

The normal occurrence for downhill lies is just the opposite of that for uphill lies. When your wedge contacts your X, it's still above the base of the ball. The bottom of the club doesn't get under the ball, so the sand propels it out fast and at a low angle. The leading edge also may actually bounce into the ball—a completely skulled shot.

As with the uphill lie, make sure you lean your body perpendicular with the slope. This will help you slap the sand with the more downward action you need to get the leading edge under the ball. If the downhill lie is steep, you'll need to move your X to about two and one-half inches behind the ball, as insurance against skulling the shot.

38 WHICH WEDGE?

The sand wedge you play can have a major effect on your results. Depending on your swing steepness and the type of sand you play from, one club may be really difficult for you to play with, whereas another design might make your sand shots amazingly easy.

The most important factors are the *degree of bounce built into the flange* and the *width of the flange*. The wider the flange is from the leading edge to the back, the more it will tend to bounce rather than dig. Also, the more degrees of bounce the flange has—that is, the degree to which the back of the flange protrudes below the leading edge—the more it will also tend to bounce. A club with both a wide flange and a high degree of bounce will work best when you're playing from soft, deep sand, because the club won't dig and leave the ball short.

Conversely, if you play from firmer sand, you don't want a club that bounces too much, because you'll skull too many shots. In this situation, you'll need a club with a narrower, more compact flange and with fewer degrees of bounce built in.

Try some practice shots with clubs that have these types of flanges and differing degrees of bounce. If you know what to look for, you'll soon find the perfect sand wedge for your game.

5 | PUTTING TO WIN

The Secrets to Mastering Golf's Ground Game

To the novice golfer who's just learning the challenges of this great game, putting must seem easy. After all, there's a nice smooth green and a four-and-one-quarter-inch cup just a few feet or so away, ready to collect that little 1.68-inch golf ball. So the novice figures that if a player can cover more than four hundred yards in just two strokes with incredible accuracy, then tapping in a four-foot putt is a sure thing.

Well, I wish I could tell you that putting is the easiest part of the game. At times, it may seem to be the case. Some days, I sink every four footer dead center. In fact, I may not miss a single putt under ten feet in an entire round. And for good measure, I drill in three or four putts in the twenty- to forty-foot range. These are the days when I shoot a round in the low 60s and make a move in the tournament.

But the curious question all players on the PGA Tour ask themselves is, "If putting can be so easy on one day, why can't it be that easy *every* day?" I'm sure you've asked yourself the same question, because almost everyone who's played the game for any length of time has experienced hot streaks that have convinced the golfer that he or she really knows how to putt. Yet the same player will have had many more days when he or she just couldn't seem to buy a putt—even a simple three footer. These are the times we all feel the most desperate, when we'll try anything, including a new putter, in an attempt to get our confidence back. To be truthful, a different model putter *can* sometimes help, particularly if its look, lie, length, and loft are better suited to you. But often putting problems have nothing to do with the equipment we use—or our stroke! I have only changed putters a very few times in my career.

At every level of the game, golfers suffer from extreme inconsistency in their results on the greens—maybe more so than in their long games. But before you start revamping your stroke and searching your local pro shop for a new putter, let me fill you in on a few things I've learned over the years that have helped me keep a positive mental outlook on the greens.

The most important thing to keep in mind is that no matter how perfectly you stroke any putt, there's no guarantee it's going to drop into the hole. You see, even a freshly cut green that looks as though it's perfectly groomed can impart many tiny bumps and jiggles to the roll of the ball. Any of them can move the ball just imperceptibly enough so that instead of dropping dead center the ball catches, say, the left center of the hole while it's turning a little to the left—just enough so that the ball spins out.

I was told that Dave Pelz, a long-time putting coach for PGA Tour players, determined that on the best putting surfaces that money can buy a device that rolls the ball exactly the same way each time does not hole every putt—even from a few feet! There will always be some imperfection, which can only be attributed to

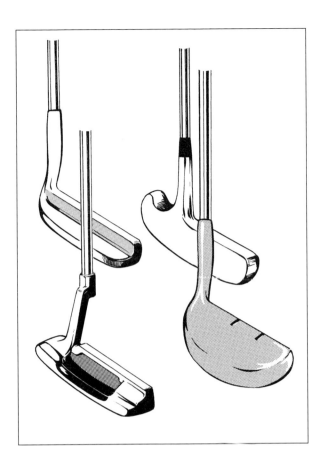

Sometimes a new putter can put a stop to a slump.

inconsistency in the putting surface, that makes a few balls stay out. Pelz also discovered that on greens that were in less-than-perfect condition, the percentage of putts made, even with a perfect roll, went down noticeably. This indicates that if you are a public course golfer or even a member of a private club with well-maintained greens, you may miss even more putts than the PGA Tour player does, simply because the greens won't let you make them. Another thing that can have a significant effect on how well you putt is the time of day you play. It's no secret on the PGA Tour that players putt, on average, a little better if they have a morning tee time than an afternoon one. Why? Because they'll be putting on greens that have fewer footprints and spike marks on them, particularly in the area extending out to about five feet around the hole. This is where every player walks and where the ball loses its speed and is most susceptible to such imperfections. If you play on a weekend after-noon at a crowded course on which players started teeing off at dawn, well, I'm sure even Tom Kite or Nick Faldo or I would often struggle too.

LEARN TO ROLL WITH THE PUNCHES

If you add all of this variability in the greens to the inaccuracies that can creep into your stroke or alignment, you can see how erratic your performance might be from one day to the next. I'd like to give you a couple of examples of just how hot—or cold—an individual player can be at one time or another.

I played in the 1982 PGA Championship, at Southern Hills in Tulsa, Oklahoma, when I was still trying to establish myself on the Tour. I had a pretty good tournament but was way behind runaway winner Ray Floyd going into the last nine holes on this very tough track. Don't ask me how, but I suddenly started making every-thing—long, short, and in-between—and I birdied the last six holes to finish in a tie for second. That finish in a major event put me on the map as a genuine Tour player, and I had my first top-twenty season the following year.

Ten years later, I had a similar run in a major; I sunk five birdies in a row (holes six through ten) during the second round of the 1992 Masters. Then, in the final round when—guess who—Ray Floyd was set to overtake me, I drained back-to-back clutch putts on the eighth and ninth holes to take control again for good.

By the same token, I've probably looked foolish—or maybe even like a choker—on the greens during other majors. At the 1985 PGA Championship at Cherry Hills in Denver, I led after a red-hot 65 in the second round in which I made everything. The next day, even though I hit the ball decently, I putted like I'd never played golf before, zoomed to a 76, and eventually wound up in third place behind Hubert Green and Lee Trevino.

Probably the most disappointing pressure putting I've ever done was again at a PGA Championship, this time in 1990 at Shoal Creek near Birmingham, Alabama. On this really demanding layout, I was having a great final round—four under through eleven holes—and had come from behind to take the lead. It was beginning to look like this was the week I would finally win the major championship that had eluded me to that point. Then at the twelfth hole, I had a fairly simple four footer for par; when the ball took a U-turn at the hole and just sat there looking at me, I was somewhat shocked, and my confidence took a jolt. On the fourteenth and fifteenth holes, I missed both greens narrowly, but chipped up nicely both times. Unfortunately, both those putts from the four-foot range went in and came back out. I went on to bogey the sixteenth as well and wound up losing to Wayne Grady by three strokes. That's one major championship I'll always feel I gave away.

My point in relating these stories is to convince you that you're not alone in the ups and downs you encounter on the greens. People say I often look a little indifferent when the putts aren't dropping (even sometimes when they are!) compared with some other players who get so mad you can almost see the steam coming out of their ears. It's not true that I'm indifferent. I've just decided that one of the best things anyone can do for himself or herself as a putter—and as a golfer in general—is to learn to roll with the punches. I try to take the bitter with the sweet.

I give every putt my best read, my best alignment, and my best stroke. After that, it's out of my hands, so I don't see why I—or you—should agonize over every putt that doesn't go in. If I'd been doing that, I'm sure I'd be a basket case by now.

Instead, my attitude of giving it my best shot and accepting the consequences has made me a much better putter over the long haul. I was really pleased to note that in the Tour putting statistics for 1992, I moved up to eighth, the highest I've ever been. Believe me, everyone on the Tour putts well. Knowing that I putted better than all but a handful of players solidifies my belief that my mental approach to putting is a good one.

If you're a very intense player, I hope you'll adopt a little more of a carefree attitude toward your results on the greens too. Mind you, when I say *carefree,* I don't mean you can become sloppy in your preparation for the stroke. I mean that once you've given a putt your best effort, learn to accept the consequences and stay positive for the next time.

Now that we've discussed the mental framework that every good putter needs, let's talk about the mechanics of the setup and stroke itself.

THE PERSONAL TOUCH

Putting is the most personal part of the game. Even among the best, no two golfers could be said to have exactly the same style. For example, Gary Player has won nine major championships with a very tense-looking setup and a pop stroke in which the putterhead makes almost no follow-through after contact. Player is also one of the few great putters who addresses the ball from an extremely closed stance. Jack Nicklaus in his prime putted from an extremely crouched position and delivered the putter squarely through the ball with a pistonlike push from his right hand and arm. Up-and-coming left-handed star Phil Mickelson exhibits a textbook one-piece arm-and-shoulder stroking action in which his hands, arms, and shoulders all move as a single unit, with no independent wrist action. These players have all made a million putts, so we know that there's no one setup or stroke style that you have to conform to to make your share of shots.

That said, there are generally considered to be two basic categories or styles of putting stroke: wristy and nonwristy. As I noted, Phil Mickelson has a firm-wristed stroking style, which is generally considered preferable because it has fewer moving parts. The putterface is basically an immovable extension of the hands and arms, which are set in motion by a back-and-forth movement of the shoulders and arms along the target line. Because the wrists stay firm, there should be no fluctuation in the angle of the putterface through impact, and the blade should remain fairly low to the ground for a nice square hit.

So theoretically, a pure arm-and-shoulder stroke would seem the best. However, there's one criticism of this style that I think is valid.

The Classic Swing of
FRED COUPLES

With the motion of the stroke coming from the shoulders alone, the stroke can feel somewhat mechanical; it's harder to develop the feel for distance that is such an important part of good putting.

On the flip side of the coin, you have the wristy style of putter. This is the player who uses some arm-and-shoulder action but also makes extensive use of the wrists in generating force to the stroke. Usually, the wristy putter's stroke covers a shorter distance going back and through than does the nonwristy putter. Also, because of the hinging of the wrists, the putterblade will come up higher at the top of the backstroke and the top of the follow-through.

There's a logical argument that when wrist action becomes predominant in the stroke, there's a greater chance for the putterhead to be turned fractionally off line as well as a chance that you might not hit the ball as squarely as with a nonwristy stroke. However, the wristy stroke does have an advantage in that it gives most players a better sense of feel for the putterhead and for the precise amount of force they should impart to the ball. I might add that a couple of players who were the best of their era exemplified the wristy style—Arnold Palmer and Billy Casper. Last time I looked, Palmer had won three more Masters than I and Casper had won two more U.S. Opens. So I'm pretty well convinced that a wristy style can work.

WHY MY SETUP AND STROKE WORK

I like to think of myself as having a natural putting style. If I had to describe my stroke, I guess I'd say it's a sort of hybrid style that's between the purely wristy and nonwristy styles. Basically, I use my arms and shoulders to generate the stroke force. However, I try to keep the stroke natural rather than rigid, and so my wrists do hinge a trifle, both at the top of the backstroke and the end of the follow-through. I feel I have a small swinging motion in my stroke.

I don't decide whether to use my wrists or not. Instead, because I hold the club quite lightly, my wrists simply respond more when I'm making the putterhead swing farther on longer putts. How much they hinge is a function of the length of putt and the amount of force needed to reach the hole. On a two footer, my wrists won't

A look at my putting setup from two angles.

hinge at all; on an uphill fifty footer, my stroke will definitely include a noticeable wrist hinge.

Before we get into how you should stroke the ball, though, let's get you set up in the right position to roll the ball smoothly on target.

The main thing I want to accomplish in setting up over the ball is to get as comfortable as possible. I think you should do the same. The purpose of getting comfortable is to keep your body in a steady position throughout the stroke. No matter what kind of stroke you choose, if you don't stay still during the stroke your chances of keeping the putter on line go way down.

I like to assume a slightly open address position—just as I do in my full swing. Lines across my toes, knees, hips, and, to a lesser degree, my shoulders would point a little left of the line the putt should roll along. In this regard I'm like a number of other top putters. It seems that from the open alignment position it's a lot easier to see the line of putt as I'm making my final adjustments before executing the stroke.

In terms of my setup, I probably stand a little farther away from the ball than average. My legs are fairly straight, with just a tiny bit of flex in the knees. However, I do bend over quite a bit from the waist, perhaps more than many Tour players. This brings my eyes pretty much directly over the line of the ball, a positioning that makes it easier to get a true reading of both my target line and the clubface alignment.

You may opt to stand a touch closer to the ball, perhaps with a little less bend from the waist. But whatever amount of bend you find is most comfortable for you, have a friend make sure your setup puts your eyes more or less over the ball and the target line. If your head is behind the ball but on the target line and you are right-eye dominant, this is perfectly permissible.

The width of your putting stance is a personal thing. For most putts, my stance is on the narrow side. However, I don't consider stance width to be a true fundamental of putting. The main thing is to get comfortable and steady. If you prefer a wider stance, that's fine. In fact, when it's windy, say during British Open week, I often widen my stance for greater stability. Don't hesitate to adjust.

In terms of positioning the ball in relation to your stance, I agree with those teachers who say to place the ball opposite a spot to the left of center in your stance (for a righty player) but not much farther forward than the inside of your left heel. The idea here is to catch the ball at or just ever so slightly after the bottom of your stroke.

On coarser Bermuda grass greens, I suggest you try something slightly different: position the ball more forward, opposite your left instep. It will allow you to contact the ball a fraction later in the stroke, when the putterhead is even more on its upswing. I believe this is a very useful setup adjustment, because it allows you to get the ball rolling with overspin as quickly as possible. The faster you can get the ball rolling with overspin, the more truly the ball will roll, particularly on this type of putting surface. If you hit down on the ball on Bermuda, the ball always seems to hop and often gets thrown off line right at the start. So set up with the ball a little more forward in your stance and your hands about even with it.

Incidentally, regarding your hands, I strongly recommend holding the club with a very light grip pressure in both hands. I don't think there's anything worse than taking a death grip on the putter, as it can only inhibit you from executing a smooth stroking action.

MAKING THE NATURAL STROKE

Once I'm set up, I take the putter back from the ball mainly with my arms and shoulders; they move back as a single unit. If anything, I'd say my left hand is more of a "guide" hand, with the right supplying more of the force. The putter stays low to the ground throughout the stroke if it's a short putt; however, the longer the stroke, the more my wrists will hinge in response to the weight of the putterhead going back. If you grip the club nice and lightly, you'll find this hinging action will take place naturally. You don't have to decide or measure how much your wrists should hinge. They just will.

Here's an analogy that will help you visualize what I mean. Imagine you're playing with a small child and you want to roll a ball on the ground just a few feet to him or her. As you roll the ball, notice how your arm controls the action with no movement of the wrist at all.

Now imagine you're rolling a ball a little farther, say fifteen feet. Notice how, in addition to the smooth swing of your arm, your wrist hinges a little bit in response to that arm swing. Now imagine yourself rolling the ball forty feet or more along the ground, and you see that your wrist hinges backward and forward at both ends of the swing even more. This is *exactly* what you should let happen in your putting stroke. You get the best of both worlds—feel for distance from the hinging of the wrists at the top of the stroke and follow-through with control of the putter through the impact zone.

As to the path of the putter, obviously you'd like to keep it mov-

A look at my putting backstroke from two angles.

A look at my putting downstroke from two angles.

ing along the target line you've chosen for as much of the stroke as possible. The reason is that staying on this path can only make your roll of putt more consistent than if you swing the putter way inside the target line on both the backswing and follow-through. In fact, some experts say you should literally force the putterhead to stay precisely on the target line throughout the entire stroke. To do this, though, you'd have to manipulate the club artificially to the top of the backstroke. Therefore, I don't agree with this approach. The longer the length of a given stroke, the more it should gradually move inside the target line on both the backstroke and follow-through—just as a full swing does. You wouldn't want to try to keep the clubhead directly on the target line for a full swing, would you? Neither should you consciously try to do so for the swing of the putter.

That said, it's best if you make a natural swing of the putterhead and still keep it fairly close to the target line to add consistency through impact. That's one reason I like to bend more from the waist than most players. With my arms hanging straight down as they do when I bend from the waist, the natural movement of the putter doesn't deviate as much from the target line at any point. My arm and shoulder movement can more easily stay close to the target line.

As I'm making the stroke, I strive to swing the putter the same distance back and through, while also keeping the tempo of the stroke about the same. Resist any tendency to hit or jab at the ball on the downstroke—stroke through the putt with a smooth, even acceleration. Some golfers find it helpful, either in practice or on the course, to count "one" during the backstroke and "two" during the downstroke to help them keep the length and tempo in both directions uniform. If that helps you, by all means do it.

There's one other thing I consciously strive for in the stroke: that's to keep my head as still as possible until after the ball is on its way. I know it sounds like a simple point, but it's not. The urge to look at the ball's movement as you're actually stroking it is very strong. Moreover, any tendency to come out of the stroke the slightest fraction early will negatively affect the aim of the putterblade.

Touring professionals have a definite advantage over amateurs regarding putting stroke discrepancies, in that they have the availability of videotapes of themselves in competition. I'm always on the lookout to see if I'm keeping my head still over my putts. You may not get to see yourself on tape, so remember this: if you have any sense that you might be moving your head during the stroke, have a friend watch you on the practice green or, better yet, during a round when you're under some tension on the greens. If your friend affirms that you're moving early, the best advice is to train yourself not to look up after the ball at all; just listen for it to drop into the hole.

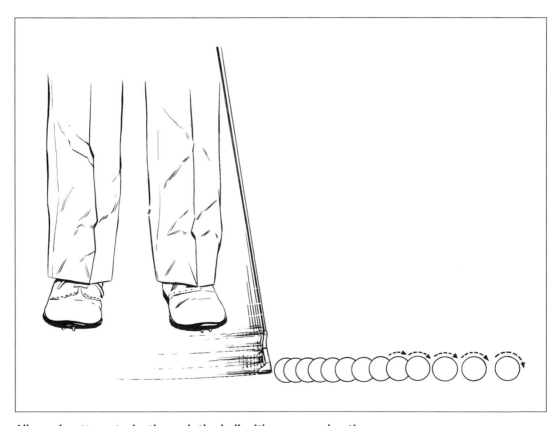

All good putters stroke through the ball with even acceleration.

THE CROSS-HANDED STYLE—
A VIABLE OPTION

We haven't talked a whole lot about how to grip the club when putting. There are a few ways to hold the putter and you may have heard of or tried many of them. Let me tell you a little bit about my own experimentation with the grip.

For almost all of my career I've used a pretty conventional putting grip—the reverse overlap, in which the index finger of the left hand overlaps the last two fingers of the right hand. And, of course, my grip is also conventional (for right handers) in that my right hand is lower than my left on the grip.

Obviously I've been successful with this style. However, I've always been one to experiment when I'm practicing. For a number of years, I've occasionally tried putting cross-handed. It wasn't really out of a major concern for the state of my putting game. In fact, as I mentioned earlier, I was wrapping up the best year statistically in putting that I've had in my career. I had just competed in Scotland in the Dunhill Cup and had played fairly well and didn't putt poorly but really just didn't make many of those ten- to twelve-foot-range birdie putts. I guess I was ready to try something fresh that would add some excitement to my putting. Sometimes changing putters will do that. The times I've putted cross-handed in practice, I didn't notice any miraculous improvement, but it wasn't all bad either.

At the last official event of the 1992 season, I was practicing before the start of the Tour Championship, played that year at the famed Pinehurst No. 2 course. Nick Price, John Cook, Davis Love, and I were all vying for Player of the Year. I started practicing some cross-handed putts on Wednesday afternoon before the first round. A fair number were going in so I kept at it. After a while I said to my caddie, Joe LaCava, "What do you think?" He said, "Freddie, the way you roll the ball that way, you ought to putt cross-handed for a whole season!" I thought about it for a while and decided, why not? On Thursday, when I showed up on the first green with my left hand below my right, I could hear my playing partner and friend Davis Love having quite a chuckle as I stood over the ball.

Well, after a fairly slow start, I shot a pair of 66s on the weekend to finish third, and I rolled the ball really nicely. Since then I've been putting cross-handed. I'm not saying I'll never change back to conventional putting. But I will say that a cross-handed style could prove helpful if you're the kind of player whose left (or lead) wrist breaks down at impact, causing you to mis-hit putts or pull them left. The cross-handed method makes it easier to keep the left wrist ahead of the club-face until after impact, which promotes on-line putts. It also seems easier for me to get my shoulders square to the line with my left hand below the right at address. I'm not as concerned about this with the full swing; in fact, my shoulders are quite a bit left when driving. But, in putting, I think shoulders square is most beneficial.

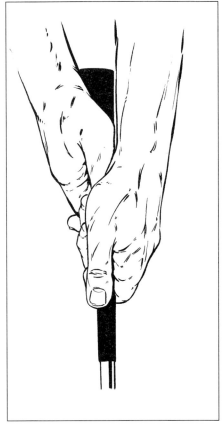

The cross-handed grip.

Aside from explaining this benefit of cross-handed putting, my point is to encourage you to listen to your intuition and not be afraid to make style changes when you're in a down cycle. It doesn't have to be a grip change. Maybe it's just a matter of widening or opening your stance, bending a bit more from the waist, or adjusting your weight distribution at address. If you're on the practice green and you find an adjustment that makes you comfortable and confident, by all means give it a try.

PLANNING YOUR PUTT— IT'S AS IMPORTANT AS THE STROKE ITSELF

From tee to green, I'd probably be classified as a medium to fast player. On the greens, however, I take more time. Now, I don't want to encourage you to be slow. But I do want to make sure you understand that your awareness of the planning factors that go into your putt are every bit as important as the quality of the stroke you put on the ball. You might have the purest stroke in the world. However, if you've misread the break, you're going to misalign the putterblade and hit the putt left or right of the hole.

Actually, the better your stroke is, the more crucial your ability to read the green becomes. This is true because if you mis-aim the putter, then make a perfect stroke, you'll miss just about every time. The player with the less-consistent stroke, meanwhile, may actually end up making a few more putts than you. Here's why:

Say you have a twenty-foot putt and you read it to break four inches to the right but in actuality it's a perfectly straight putt. Then you go ahead and make a perfect stroke. Unless you get a lucky bounce, you'll miss it every time by four inches to the left.

Learning to read the different curves, or breaks, on the green will make you a more proficient putter.

Suppose another player makes the same incorrect read, but his or her stroke is not quite as precise as yours. For every putt that player hits right where planned, he or she may pull one a few inches to the left or push one a bit to the right. When such a player aims slightly left, then pushes the putt a touch, it should go in. When the player misreads the putt in this manner and then pulls it a bit, it's no big deal—he or she misses the hole by a few inches more, that's all. Meanwhile, the player's made one more putt than you did because two slight errors on one putt balanced each other off. However, trust me, if you have a sound stroke you'll make more in the long run, and especially when you need to.

I hope you're convinced that it's important not only to make a consistent stroke but to make your best read every time too. Try to take in all the information you can about your putt, starting when you're walking up to the green. Be alert to the lay of the land surrounding the green. If you play in a fairly hilly to mountainous region, many times the land surrounding the green will fall away in one direction or the other. This can create an optical illusion regarding any slope in the green itself. Say, for example, the green is built into a hillside where the ground slopes sharply from left to right. As you walk onto the green, you might think it's level; but chances are it slopes to the right more than it looks. The reason you might not see it is there's a contrast between the green itself and the left-to-right slope surrounding it. Since you see this contrast you think the green is flat; but it still can be sliding left to right along with the natural contours, and in fact it probably is. You can see this best before you actually get to the green, so when playing in a hilly area, stay alert to this.

Once on the green, look for its general slope along the line that runs from your ball to the hole. Keep in mind that no two putts are alike. As you assess the break, also note if the putt is uphill or downhill and whether the height and texture of the grass will make the putt fast or slow.

Reading a putt is a "marriage" of the contours of the ground and the speed of the putt. You can't look at a putt with a certain amount of slope and automatically decide that it will break, say, six inches to the right. The speed factors will increase the break in some cases, reduce it in others.

Say, for example, that a putt with about a six-inch break is slightly downhill on a fast surface. In this case, you'll stroke the putt more lightly than normal so the ball won't roll way past if it misses. Because on this quick downhill putt the ball will be rolling with less speed, the force of gravity (from the slope) will have a greater effect; that is, the ball will break *more* from left to right. So you may need to play ten, twelve, maybe even fifteen inches of break in this instance.

On the other hand, you may see a putt with the same degree of left-to-right slope; however, this putt is slightly uphill on a slow green. You'll need to give the ball a pretty firm rap for it to reach the hole. In doing so, the ball will roll along its line with much more speed, thus it will be less affected by the slope. So instead of playing a six-inch break for normal speed, you'll probably have to estimate only a tiny break—one or two inches—for this particular putt.

DON'T FORGET THE GRAIN

An additional factor to consider (on some putting surfaces more than others) is the grain of the green. Grain simply means the direction in which the grass is growing. It's a bigger factor in the southern parts of the United States, where the greens are usually Bermuda grass. Bermuda greens have a much stronger grain effect than do the bent grass greens that predominate in the northern and central parts of the country.

You can check the green in general by the way the grain is lying. If you're not sure, check around the hole. If you notice that one side of the hole looks worn, then the grain is growing *toward* the worn side and you have to add a grain factor to the break you've read. *Other grain checkpoints:* the grain will usually run toward any substantial body of water nearby, or it will grow toward the setting sun.

Get in the habit of taking a look at your line of putt from both sides of the cup, rather than just from ball to hole. (By the way, it's good to do this soon after you reach the green, while your playing partners are also getting ready, to save time.) Sometimes you'll look at a putt from behind the ball and read a certain amount of break; then you'll look at it from behind the hole, and it'll appear quite different. I know it would be easy to say you should just look at the line from ball to hole and leave it at that, but many times, looking from the opposite perspective has tempered my opinion, and an adjustment in aligning the putt has paid off.

Understand that I'm not telling you that looking at the putt from hole to ball is better than looking at it from ball to hole. I am suggesting you respect both perspectives. Examine the line from the ball to the hole and get your first impression. Then look at the putt from the opposite angle. If both angles look identical, you're all set. If the ball-to-hole angle shows, say, an eight-inch break but the reverse angle shows a little less, maybe you should adjust slightly and play a six-inch break. Unfortunately, there's no formula for this. My best advice is to take the information from both outlooks together, then decide on the final line and stroke the ball decisively along that line.

SPEED KILLS

Once I've made my read and set up to the ball, I have a clear picture in my mind about how the ball will roll along the intended line, take the anticipated break, and drop sweetly into the cup.

With respect to speed, I probably relate more to Jack Nicklaus's style of "dying" the ball in the hole than to either Arnold Palmer or Tom Watson who, during their primes, banged the ball into the cup. Palmer and Watson both went after every putt, because when they were at their best they knew they'd make any four footers coming back. I don't want to criticize their approach because Palmer and Watson were two of the greatest putters in history. However, those four-footers coming back are not my personal favorites. Moreover, if they don't go in, they really take a toll on your mental game.

The best thing you can do for your putting is to work very hard to get control of your speed and have a good enough stroke that you can hit the ball solidly every time. So, from twenty-five feet or less, you can either hole out or hit the ball within easy tap-in range.

Of course, there's another school of thought that says you'll make more putts if you go after them a little more aggressively. The basic idea is that if the ball is moving with a little more speed, it's likely to hold a truer line, particularly in those last few feet around the hole where it's likely to be a bit bumpier. This is a reasonable point. However, I think in the long run, the closer to the hole you leave your first putt, the better off you'll be. Also, you'll come out at least even on how many first putts you sink, because more of your slower-rolling putts will fall in the side door.

Keep in mind that developing the kind of touch I've recommended will take practice. Go to the putting green every chance you get. On occasion you should practice a different putt with every stroke, so you constantly have to adjust your perception of distance. Remember that with the exception of short putts, distance, not direction, should be your primary focus. If you keep striving to perfect the speed of your putts, the number of putts you take per round should gradually start going down.

WHAT ABOUT ROUTINE?

You hear a lot of coaching about having an exact series of steps in setting up to the putt and that you should use religiously a specific preputt routine. The theory is that if all your setup moves follow a pattern, so will your stroke. Well, to tell you the truth, it sounds like a good idea. However, I've never made up an outline of exact moves to perform before putting, and I wouldn't advise you to spend an inordinate amount of time on this either. Chances are that I—and you—will develop a pattern without even knowing or planning it. But there are too many little things that can happen from one putt to the next, and I think it is counterproductive to be too set and stiff in your movements. I'd rather see you spend your practice time working on building a smooth-tempo, natural stroke;

developing your green-reading ability; honing a super feel for speed; and letting your comfortable routine fall into place.

Last, don't forget to keep a carefree attitude about your putting. I know it sounds like a contradiction to ask you to work hard at something, then be carefree about it, but this is really one of my secrets. The point is to do the best you can on every stroke, then take an accepting attitude toward the results. As time goes by, you'll realize that this is the best approach to putting well.

COUPLES'S CLINIC

39 WHEN IN DOUBT, PLUMB BOB

There may be times when your normal green-reading process doesn't provide you with the clear and certain image of the break you want. If so, I recommend that you try the plumb bob method of reading the break. Here's how.

Stand behind the ball so that you could draw a perfectly straight line from your dominant eye through the ball and to the cup. Make sure to stand so that your shoulders are parallel to the horizon.

Next, hold the putter grip in front of you between your thumb and forefinger, so that the clubshaft hangs in a perfect vertical plane. Line up so the clubshaft "covers" the ball. Close your nondominant eye. If the shaft is now covering the hole, this means the putt should roll straight. If the clubshaft seems to align to the left of the hole, the plumb bob indicates that the ground falls off to the right and the putt will break that way. If the putter shaft aligns to the right of the cup, it means the putt will break to the left.

Two notes:

1. You really only need to use the plumb bob method when the putt is straight or close to straight. You should be able to notice substantial breaks in either direction without this method.

2. You need to be sure you know which of your eyes is dominant. To determine this, hold an index finger up in line with some object. Now close your left eye. Did the object appear to move? If so, your left eye is dominant. If the object appeared to stay in place, it's your right eye that's dominant.

40 THE RIGHT GRIP PRESSURE

I believe in maintaining a relatively light grip pressure for all shots, including putts. The tighter you grip the handle, the less feel for the putterhead you'll have during the stroke. And I think you need to retain all the feel you can, particularly on long putts.

On short putts, for which you don't need as much distance feel, a little firmer grip is fine. However, as the putts get longer, I tend to grip lighter and lighter with my right hand. This light grip pressure makes it easier for the right wrist to hinge, as I'd like it to on the longer strokes.

As you get into putts of twenty-five feet and longer, gradually lighten your right-hand grip pressure and allow that right wrist to hinge and unhinge naturally at the top of the stroke. The faster the greens you play on, the more this should help your distance control. With a reasonable amount of practice, your percentage of three-putt greens should gradually diminish—I hope to zero.

41 THE "ANTI-YIPS" METHOD

I'm told there's no more helpless feeling in golf than to step up to a simple two- or three-foot putt, and *know* there's no way you're going to make it. I used the words *I'm told* because, fortunately, I've never gotten this negative over short putts. And I hope I never will. To ensure that this never happens, I employ a little different technique on the short ones, which I refer to as the "anti-yips" method. Here's how it works:

First, grip the club a bit tighter than you would on medium or long putts. Not a death grip, just a little firmer. This will help produce a low, on-line stroke that will keep the ball moving to the hole.

Once you're lined up and ready, I recommend that you stroke these short ones rather firmly into the back of the cup, instead of dying them in. Why? The short, firm stroke from inside three feet takes away a bit of the guesswork. From this distance and with a firm stroke, you can play virtually every putt as straight in. You'll only have to adjust for break (and only slightly at that) if there's a pronounced slope and the green is slick.

A session or two of specifically practicing short putts using my method should really help you if you've been getting tentative to the point of getting a case of the yips. Here's a practice session tip (which you can also use during actual play): imagine a pair of hands about a foot behind the hole, positioned so that they're encircling the back of the cup. Determine to stroke the ball right into the center of those hands. This image can help remove any pressure you may be feeling, and you'll stroke the ball firmly, right in the middle of the cup.

42 ALL WORN OUT

I grew up playing on a municipal course in the Seattle area that always got a pretty heavy amount of play. The more play a course gets, the more you need to be aware that the green will be most worn within a five-foot-diameter circle around the hole.

Check around the hole intently as you're looking over your medium- or longer-length putts. If the ball hits an exceptionally worn-down area as it's rolling toward the cup, it can pick up a bit of extra speed. Instead of dying within "gimme" range, it's more likely to trickle a bit farther by—leaving you a little work coming back over a rough putting area.

So when the area around the hole is worn, develop an image of feeding the ball into that five-foot circle, so the ball will trickle up to (or into) the hole, instead of sliding past.

43 FORWARD PROGRESS

One of the main stroke problems of high handicap amateurs is that they decelerate the putterhead at impact. (It happens on Tour, too.) I believe the principal reason for deceleration is simply anxiety on the player's part about making a just-right stroke. Instead of letting the stroke flow through impact, the player gets tentative and tries to steer the putter through. The result: the putterhead wavers and the ball slides off line or the ball never reaches the hole at all.

The problem is really a mental one, and here's a tip that I've found very useful in correcting it. Set up to your putt with the ball positioned normally in your stance. Next, imagine there's a second ball placed two inches (toward the target) in front of the real one. Now, accelerate the putterhead smoothly through the imaginary ball, sending it straight into the hole.

If you concentrate on doing this, you'll forget about the real ball and lose your anxiety over hitting it just right. You'll automatically stroke right through it to stroke that second ball as well.

Try using this "forward progress" method, and you'll start hitting your putts with the acceleration you need to keep the ball on line and to reach the hole every time.

44 USE YOUR IMAGINATION

You may play a course that challenges you with extremely quick, sloped putting surfaces. Conversely, the main task might be to get it there on slow greens.

If your greens are on either side of mid-speed range, start using your imagination to adjust to differing speeds. Say you have a really quick downhill, down-grain fifteen footer, like one you might see the pros working on at Augusta National during the Masters. In this case, imagine the hole is two feet *closer* to you than it really is, then try to hit your putt into this imaginary hole. By doing this, you'll be easing your ball down toward the real hole so that if it doesn't drop, it should finish within tap-in range instead of sliding past.

On the other hand, when the putt is slow, uphill, and/or against the grain, you really need to be firm. Often, you'll hit what you think is a really solid putt, and you're amazed to see that it still pulls up short. To counteract this tendency, imagine that the hole is a full two feet farther away than it actually is. Then remind yourself to execute an aggressive stroke that will make the ball reach this imaginary target. By doing so, you greatly increase your chances of reaching the real cup instead of pulling up maddeningly short. Even if the ball is moving a little fast as it reaches the real hole, it's still likely to drop because, when the putt's uphill, the back of the hole is higher than the front so the ball will tend to dive in.

Using your imagination in this way will definitely help you make more putts.

45 WHEN IT'S WET, WHEN IT'S WINDY

Keep in mind that wet or windy conditions don't affect only your long game. They can wreak havoc with your putting, too. However, if you understand how to adjust, you'll be one up on most of the competition.

WET GREENS

In rainy conditions, the greens naturally soak up the moisture. Everyone understands that this makes the greens slower, so you need a longer stroke to cover the distance. What a lot of amateurs don't realize is that on wet greens the ball will also break less than normal.

There's simply more resistance to the force of gravity when there's moisture on the grass blades then when they're dry. Also, because you're stroking harder to reach the hole, for most of the way to the hole the ball's rolling faster than normal; this helps it resist the break.

My tried-and-true rule of thumb is that if the greens are wet, I plan on the ball breaking *no more than* half as much as normal. If on a dry green the ball would break a foot, I play no more than a six-inch break. If there would usually be a four-inch break, I play for no more than two inches of curve, starting the ball inside the high lip of the hole. If you do this too, you'll make a lot more putts.

WINDY CONDITIONS

I think most Tour pros, including me, would tell you that one of the hidden difficulties of playing in wind is that it makes putting so much tougher. First, it dries out the greens, making them faster and causing putts to break more. Even more significantly, a stiff wind can easily throw you off balance during the stroke and affect the ball's line.

When the wind is strong, you're probably better off giving up a bit of feel by gripping the putter a little more firmly. This encourages a more arms-only stroking action and keeps the putterhead low to the ground. Also, widening your stance will give your body greater stability.

Remember that a substantial breeze behind you can carry a putt farther and that a head wind can make the ball pull up quicker than you might think. Adjust accordingly.

Last, experiment with addressing the ball and do not ground the putter. On fast greens on windy days, I think this adjustment is a great help.

46 AT GREAT LENGTH

Although I've never used a long putter (a putter forty-eight inches or more in length) in competition, I think it is worth considering, if the five-feet-and-in range is your weakest area. The positive point about the long putter is that by "splitting" the hands when you grip—so that the right hand makes the stroke while the left hand plays a supporting role—you promote a rhythmical, slow stroke with no chance of breaking down at the ball. This is what you want on a short putt. You'll rarely see a quick, jabbing stroke by a player who has confidence around the hole.

Of course, you want to make a smooth, even-tempo stroke on virtually all putts with any length putter. But I've noticed in Pro-Ams—particularly in older players—that a smooth, even tempo on medium- and especially short-range putts is tough to come by. That's why I recommend you experiment with a long putter if your short putts are more of a problem than your long ones. You might even become automatic from five feet and in.

47 WELCOME CHANGES

Most often when handicap players work on a practice green, they'll use three or four balls, hitting each from the same spot before moving on to another hole.

There's a better way to practice. That's to take just one ball and hit each putt just one time. Why? Because it *forces* you to read each putt individually, just as you must on the course.

The next time you practice putting, drop one ball on the

green, then read and stroke a left-to-right twenty footer, then a thirty-foot downhiller with a little right-to-left break, and so on. Putt eighteen holes in a row in this fashion, making sure no two putts are identical.

I think you'll see that after a while, when you go out in actual play, your green-reading skills will have increased. With that increase, the number of putts you take will decrease.

48 FIND THE SWEET SPOT

One of the most overlooked factors in good putting is to strike the ball consistently at the putterface's center of percussion, more commonly known as the "sweet spot." This is the point on the clubface at which, when the ball is stroked, there is no off-centeredness that causes the clubface to twist off line.

Most golfers assume that the sweet spot is at the dead-center point between the putterhead's toe and heel ends. This assumption is reinforced by the fact that manufacturers often place an alignment mark, usually a small line, at the top center of the putterhead. However, the center point of the clubface and the sweet spot aren't always identical. Here's how to find the true center of percussion.

Hold your putter vertically above and in front of you by the handle (suspended with just your thumb and forefinger), so the putterhead is at eye level and can swing freely. Take a golf tee in your other hand and *tap* the clubface with the pointed end. If the putterhead twists at all (you can feel it in your thumb and forefinger), you haven't hit the exact center of percussion. When the putterhead rebounds straight back, you have.

Note whether the center of percussion is at a point different from the marked center of the putterface. More often than not, the center of percussion will be slightly toward the heel side of the putterface. That's because the heel side also has the weight of the shaft and hosel attached to it. You may want to put your own mark at the top of the putterhead, using paint or a magic marker to identify the true sweet spot.

49 ONE ON ONE

When it's time to play, the best way to approach putting is to simplify your thoughts. Pick out one useful setup or stroke key for the day, rather than confuse yourself with a number of them. As long as all the putting keys you have to choose from are sound, you'll probably benefit from any one of them on a given day.

I use different single putting keys all the time—I just settle on one that seems particularly helpful or vivid as I'm warming up on the practice green. Here are several putting keys to consider before making your individual selection:

- *Grip lightly.* Keep tension from building in the hands and arms by focusing on holding the putter grip lightly—especially with the left hand.
- *Ball forward.* Position the ball off the left instep to help catch the ball slightly on the upswing and obtain the truest overspin.
- *Accelerate the putter.* Keep the putterhead moving well past impact by stroking an imaginary second ball that lies in front of the real one.
- *Perfect alignment.* By carefully aligning the putterface at address, you greatly increase your chances of sinking the putt.
- *Still head.* Imagine that your head is being held lightly in place by a friend's hands, until well after the ball has begun its roll.

50 BE CAREFREE

Most golfers put a lot of extra pressure on themselves on the greens, whatever their level of play. They tell themselves, "I've got to make this putt"—whether it's to win the U.S. Open, to advance in their club championship, or even to win a two-dollar "Nassau." I think, oftentimes, this self-imposed pressure hurts golfers more than it helps—at all levels.

I don't believe you can *make* yourself employ a better stroke by thinking about the importance of what's at hand. It may sound simple, but I think you should just try to make the best read you can; the best alignment of the putterface you can; and then the most relaxed, yet sound, stroke you can on every single putt. Then simply accept the consequences. The ball is either going to drop or it isn't. You may have made an absolutely perfect read and stroke and never even realized it, because the ball hit a spike mark right after it started rolling and bounced off line. On the other hand, sometimes a putt you should have missed will roll over some kind of imperfection that influences it just enough to make it fall into the hole. Most golfers don't acknowledge that can happen, but the breaks work both ways.

I really believe you'll be a better putter over the long haul if you learn to take a carefree approach to your game on the greens. Golf is meant to be played for fun. Give your ball the very best roll you can. Then if you have to putt it again, putt it again. And after you miss one, sure, think about why you missed it, but just for a matter of seconds. The best thing I can tell you after that is forget it—it's over! Then go on to the next tee and try to make a good swing.

If you play every stroke this way, you'll be learning to let your instincts do the job without the interference of imagined, external pressure. Take the good with the bad on the greens, and you'll always wind up with your best net result.

6 | **GREAT ESCAPES**

A Vivid Imagination and Subtle Swing Changes Are the
Secrets to Recovering from Tough Course Situations

This, obviously, is not the first golf instruction book ever written. There have been literally hundreds published, containing theories on what's required to groove a perfect swing, to produce wonderful golf shots, and to shoot pro-level par scores. Trends in the golf swing come and go, and this is vividly reflected in the way swings have changed over the years on the PGA Tour.

Despite the sincerest efforts of the most highly qualified teachers—in the United States and worldwide—I firmly believe this rather fatalistic statement: the golf swing will *never* be perfected. No player will ever come down the pike who, during every round, will pound every drive down the fairway, then hit all eighteen greens in regulation. At the peak of his career, Jack Nicklaus couldn't do that, and at more or less the peak of my career, I can't do it either.

Despite all the work they put into their games, the world's greatest players understand this. They realize that simply maintaining a high standard of ball striking isn't enough to win championships. Because every swing falters now and then and weather conditions alter the course of play, winning is usually determined by who, among those who struck the ball well, also managed to *scramble* the best. Most Hall of Fame–level players are (or were) truly great escape artists as well as great club swingers. Among them, Seve Ballesteros, Tom Watson, Arnold Palmer, and Lee Trevino come quickly to mind.

No matter at what level you currently play the game, there's no greater advantage than to develop a reputation as an expert trouble player. It's great to be the guy or gal in your foursome who's known for getting that impossible pitch out of the deep rough, up over a bunker, stopping it near the hole, and then canning the putt for par. If you can become an on-course Houdini, you not only will never be out of a hole but also will have a big psychological edge over your opponents, who'll be constantly worried about how you might steal another hole from them. I often feel like a great save can keep my round going as much or better than a birdie or an eagle.

WHY YOU MUST STAY COOL IN JAIL

The test of a golfer's mettle comes when he or she is up against the wall or "in jail"—in a seemingly hopeless position in which par seems out of the question and triple bogey seems closer to reality. Most of the time it's easier to be cool when you've got a straightforward nine-iron shot from the fairway on a par four or you're gunning for the green in two on a long par five. It's a lot harder to stay on an even keel when you've just made a bad swing, you've gotten a poor bounce to boot, and it looks as if you have *no* shot at all.

Yet this is the most important time to give the next shot your very best analysis and execution. In effect, the stakes are now higher than for the routine short-iron approach from the fairway. Sure, you want to do your best on every stroke. But from deep trouble, the difference between a top-class recovery and a compounded error on the next shot can mean a difference of three or four strokes on just that one hole. In addition, if you do suffer a big number at that point, it can cause you to lose confidence—and more strokes—later in the round. So you can easily move from a potentially good eighteen-hole score to a terrible one in short order, unless you develop composure in these crucial situations.

If you ever hope to become a real shotmaker, the kind of golfer who scores better than he or she swings, you have to develop a strong and creative mental approach to trouble play. What this boils down to, really, is having the awareness to see all the recovery options available, choosing the right shot under the given circumstances, and, finally, executing the shot as planned.

An awful lot of amateurs don't become recovery artists because they don't accurately judge the prestroke conditions that determine how they need to play a given shot. For example, let's say you've driven the ball into some trees. There's one tree that's right in the path of your recovery and you have to decide whether to go over it or under it. On the surface, maybe it looks like the odds of hitting the ball over the tree are better than staying under it. However, you haven't yet considered the lie. Your ball is sitting in fairly deep rough. This means it'll be almost impossible to get the ball up, because the tall grass tends to make it hard to get the ball to spin and go up. Better look more closely at that option of keeping the shot low!

Conversely, say you're in a similar position, except that the tree is a little shorter and this time you have a tight hardpan lie. Because the tree is lower, you might be more tempted to take it over the top. However, it's equally as tough for any player to get the ball up quickly from a hardpan lie because you can't get under it. You probably should look to the low road for your escape from this type of lie, too, but this time you can curve it left or right because the grass won't intervene.

In short, learn to consider every factor and every option. Suppose you're blocked out from your target and have to make a choice between playing a big hook or a big slice. Which type of curve do you naturally execute better? That's only the first point to consider. Which way is the wind blowing? It may be blowing right to left, so it will help you if your more natural shot is a draw. However, if the wind is right to left and you're better at fading the ball, the wind factor means you'll either have to slice it a lot more or go with the right-to-left shot even though it's not your strong suit. Or you may decide the odds against the shot are too great and that you should just make sure to hit the ball safely out sideways to the open fairway and take your lumps.

What kinds of penalties do you face if you try for the gambling recovery and fail to pull it off? This rightfully should be a big factor in your thinking. Let's say you're in the woods to the right of the fairway and the only chance you have to get to the green calls for a big slice. Your lie is good so you can put some sidespin on it. However, there's a lake guarding the left side of the fairway and the green. If you hit the shot straight instead of slicing it, you'll be in the drink. Do you go for it? Maybe you should purposely hit short of the green—and the water—and play for the pitch-and-putt par.

Suppose, however, you were in the same position and, instead of water guarding the left side of the green, you just had a single bunker. In this case, particularly if you're a respectable bunker player, you should go for the big slice recovery. The penalty for not pulling the shot off is not too great.

Another important factor in developing "escapability" is to know your shotmaking strengths and weaknesses. In general, when in trouble, play the shots you play best. You should rarely if ever try to escape via a shot you're not confident in—and *never* if the penalty for a miss is severe. For example, if you normally hit the ball fairly low, don't expect suddenly to produce a superhigh shot that will easily clear a dense stand of trees. If you know you don't put a lot of backspin on the ball, don't shoot straight for a pin that's tucked into a small, tightly guarded corner. Pick your spots. Know when it's within *your* capabilities to pull off a certain recovery and when to settle for a more conservative approach.

In summary, stay cool and look at all the variables every time you encounter trouble.

USE *YOUR* TYPE OF CONCENTRATION

In playing from trouble as well as from normal lies, you'll think and execute best if you work out of the concentration mode that's best for you. When I refer to a *concentration mode,* I mean you should be aware of the type of attention span you apply to the game as you work your way around the course.

You may have a temperament similar to Jack Nicklaus and Nick Faldo, who have long-term concentration. They basically stay in their game from before the first tee shot until the final putt is holed. When they're playing their best, they rarely stop between shots to kibitz with the gallery, chat with other players, or talk to their caddies about a business commitment they have after the round. It's great if you can block everything out and just think golf for about four hours like Jack and Nick, but they're an exception.

In contrast, you may be more like Lee Trevino or Fuzzy Zoeller, who are great examples of effective short-term concentrators. They usually talk to everybody on the golf course about everything—except for that one minute or so while they're assessing and executing the next shot. Then they are as serious as they come. But they understand that if they tried to force themselves to think about golf strategy every second, with their more nervous natural personalities, they'd blow a fuse in short order. Lee and Fuzzy really use their mental makeup during competition to perfection.

Every golfer should find his or her own comfortable concentration zone. Just make sure that from the moment you begin your approach to the ball, assess all your shotmaking variables, and start your setup that you've cleared out *everything* from your mind except the stroke you're about to play.

GREAT ESCAPES

Having covered the mental side of trouble play, I'll devote the remainder of this chapter to explaining exactly how to alter your setup and swing mechanics to pull off some "great escapes."

The Hard Hook

You've put the ball behind some trees and have decided your best chance of recovering is to hit a hard hook, keeping the ball low and running it onto the green. What adjustments should you make? First, always align the leading edge of the clubface squarely with the place where you want the ball to finish. This should be true whether you're trying to play a hook, slice, or straight ball. Second, align your feet, knees, hips, shoulders, and your grip so they're all set well right of your ultimate target. Your body should be aimed

In hitting a hard hook, the toe of the clubhead must lead its heel through impact.

far enough right to start the ball safely around the obstacle before beginning to hook back in. Third, move the ball a little farther back in your stance, say just in front of center, instead of opposite the left heel. This will help you contact the ball with the clubhead moving from inside the target line, adding to the draw effect. Fourth, grip the club very lightly and take plenty of club, so your hands and wrists can be a little more active during the release.

Once you've set up as described, you can pretty much make your normal swing, with only one difference. As you start down, exaggerate the releasing action of your right hand and left arm fold. This will cause the club's toe end to lead its heel and ensure that right-to-left hookspin is imparted on the ball.

Practice these setup and through-impact swing adjustments so you'll know how much draw or hook to expect on the shot.

Sidehill, Uphill, and Downhill

Many of you play in regions of the country where most of the courses have hilly terrain. And few people realize how many shots are missed based on the unevenness of the lie. Let's make sure you're clear on the adjustments you need to counteract these odd stances. Remember that for all of them a more controlled swing and maintaining balance will be crucial points.

Ball above Feet

The "baseball bat" position is the one in which the ball is far above your feet on a sidehill lie, so you feel like you're swinging at a pitch that's about knee-high. Here's how to adjust for good contact:

1. Choke down on the club to compensate for the fact that the ball is closer to you than it would be from level ground.
2. Take a club less than the distance would normally call for (because of the lower hooking trajectory of this shot).
3. Align yourself a bit right of your target, since the flatter plane of your swing causes a closing of the clubface, which results in a pull or hook shot.

4. Play the ball a bit farther back in your stance, which counteracts the tendency to hit this shot fat.

Ball below Feet

When you're standing on a sidehill lie, above the ball, the tendency is to fail to stay down, so you either hit a low slice or top the ball.

To counteract this tendency, bend slightly more than usual from the waist, take plenty of club, and align just a bit left of target, since, if anything, this shot will fade slightly. From this setup, swing normally, concentrating on good balance. Take more club than you normally would so you won't be tempted to swing hard, and you'll also maintain your balance better.

Uphill Lies

Uphill lies should be the easiest of the uneven lies to play. The ball is sitting there, ready to be launched easily skyward. If there's any problem with this position, it's that most amateurs forget that because the ground is angling upward more loft will be added to the ball's trajectory, causing it to fly *shorter* than normal. To compensate, use at least one or, more likely, two clubs longer than normal, while making a smooth, controlled, in-balance swing.

Play the ball at your normal position or a touch forward. Also, remember that sweeping the ball off an uphill lie is somewhat like sweeping a driver off a high tee. If anything, there's more tendency to draw the ball, so aim a touch right of your target.

Taming the Downhill Lie

A great many handicap players approach a severe downhill lie with as much relish as they would a hissing snake. But you can handle it by making these adjustments.

1. Move the ball back in your stance—the steeper the lie, the farther you move it back; for a really steep downhill lie, the ball could be placed behind the center of your stance, with your hands well ahead at address.

2. Align yourself for a slight fade, that is, slightly left of your target.

3. Depending on the severity of the slope, select one or two clubs *shorter* than normal, since the ball will shoot off the downhill lie at a lower, "hotter" trajectory.

4. Make a compact swing with little weight shift, focusing on maintaining a very still head.

5 Swing down along the slope and low through and past the ball. Never try to lift the ball in the air as many high handicappers do.

Remember that even with clean contact, this shot will fly low, so don't try for a miracle shot that has to carry a hazard that tightly guards the pin. Instead, plan to run the ball onto the fat part of the green if possible.

The Banana Slice

To slice the ball around trees to a tightly guarded pin placement, which is one of my favorite shots, your setup adjustments should be just the opposite of those for a hook. Once again, align your leading edge square to your ultimate target. This time, open your body alignment so that lines drawn across your toes, knees, hips, and shoulders point well left of your eventual target; your grip should be in alignment with your other body parts (that is, turned slightly left on the club handle). The more you need to slice the ball, the more you align left.

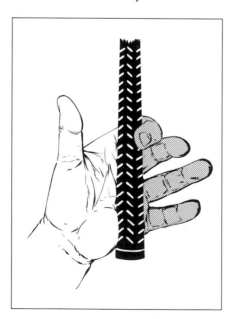

Grip the club more firmly in your left hand when playing a banana slice.

Once you've made these adjustments, the swinging action itself is as normal. One additional tip is to grip the club a bit more tightly than usual in your left hand. This is because you don't want much counterclockwise forearm rotation to occur through the impact zone. Rather, you want to hold the clubface open in relation to your body alignment. A firmer grip in the left hand (for the right-handed player) keeps that hand and forearm dominant and prevents the right hand from turning the clubface over. I often think of my sand shot action, which I described earlier, for this one.

Because you're aiming left, you'll naturally take the club away more outside the target line than normal and also return it with the face very open to the target line. Thus you'll strike the ball with a glancing blow, imparting clockwise or slice spin to the ball. Again, practice to see how much left-to-right curve you can expect from this altered setup.

One final note: remember that when you play a slice, the ball will slide off the open clubface in a higher, softer trajectory and will also land more softly. Adjust your club selection accordingly, taking at least one more club than the distance would usually call for.

Stymied? Try Hitting Off Your Knees

Since I've coached you throughout this book on the value of a loose wrist and arm hinge on your full swing, you might be able to pull off a shot that has saved me a number of times. When you've hit a wild one into the trees and can't take your normal stance, see if you can kneel on one or both knees and get enough of the ball to hit it for some yardage. The keys are to take a more lofted iron (six through nine iron) and use an extra-loose cocking of your arms and wrists on the backswing and through swing. An added benefit is that practicing this shot reinforces a round rotation of your shoulders and a very loose arm swing. One final tip: If you rehearse this shot enough and have confidence in hitting it, remember Craig Stadler; don't use a towel to kneel on. A higher laundry bill will be better than the penalty.

Cheating the Wind

I'm basically a high-ball hitter. And I don't believe in making radical changes in my setup and swing to adjust for shots into a stiff wind. Whether you hit the ball high, low, or at a medium trajectory, I'd rather not see you make big changes when hitting into the wind either. You don't want to make such radical adjustments that you mis-hit the shot entirely. The most important thing to accomplish into a head wind is just to hit the ball solidly.

I usually take a little more club to avoid hitting the shot full and causing the ball to "upshoot" in the wind. This is caused by creating too much backspin off a middle- or short-iron hit with a lot of clubhead speed. I choke down slightly on the grip position. I play the ball back in my stance.

To hit a good wind cheater shot, swing the club at less than full speed.

I think about making a nice clearing motion to the left with my hips and legs on the downswing so that my hands will arrive at the ball slightly earlier than normal and thereby shut down the loft of the club at impact. To visualize what I'm talking about, picture Lee Trevino at impact.

One last thought on the wind cheater shot: I don't like to deloft the club by hitting down on the ball and into the ground. If you're able to execute the downswing motion that I just described you should hit this shot with the same shallow swing path you make on all full shots. The more you hit down on the ball the more chance the ball will upshoot.

Battling the Borderline Lie

Every now and then you'll hit a nice drive, only to find as you approach your ball that it's come to rest smack against the left-hand edge of the rough. Assuming you're a right-handed golfer, this can be a real problem. Why? Because as you take the club away from and back into the ball on the backswing and downswing, the clubhead will move inside the target line, through the rough. It can easily get caught in either direction and throw your shot awry. (*Note:* if you play left-handed, the same effect occurs when your ball stops at the right-hand edge of the fairway.)

Here's how to counteract this tricky lie. First, stand a little closer to the ball than normal. This will encourage a more upright take-away and downswing. When you start the backswing, take the club straight back from the ball and up even more than usual. Continue to swing your arms into a high top-of-backswing position. On the downswing, pull the club down and through the ball on the same steep angle, so that the clubhead approaches from more directly behind the ball and doesn't catch in the rough.

The result of this upright swing and steep downswing will be an abbreviated follow-through and one of the few times there will be a sizable divot. This shot will tend to fly low and take a long bounce on the green and then check up.

Pine Needle Precautions

At many courses in the southeastern United States, pine trees leave a cover of pine needles on the ground, rather than normal rough. This is particularly true at Augusta National, site of the Masters. Usually the ball sits up pretty well on pine needles, so you can contact the ball cleanly. The danger in the shot is that if you ground the club, the pine needles underneath the ball may shift, causing the ball to move and you to incur a one-stroke penalty.

To prevent this possibility, always set up carefully to a ball resting on pine needles. *Never* ground your club. Rather, let it dangle a bit above and behind the ball. Assume a stance that's a tad wider than normal to provide you with maximum stability.

From here, you'll want to make a controlled swinging motion dominated by your arms, with a little less weight shift than normal. Concentrate on keeping your head still through and past impact.

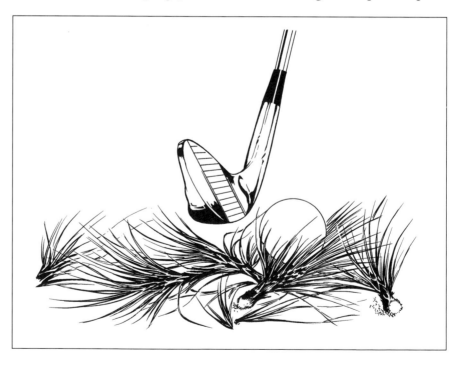

When playing a shot off pine needles, dangle the clubhead above the ground; this will prevent you from moving the ball before you swing and from being penalized one stroke.

Finally, because you'll be making a more compact swing than normal, play it smart and take one club longer than normal for the distance.

The Kikuyu Blast

If you play golf on the West Coast of the United States, you'll likely face a particular kind of rough known as Kikuyu grass. This thick steel wool–like rough is especially tough to play green-side recoveries from, since the coarse grass tends to snuff the clubhead—and thus the ball—quite readily. Sometimes, if you swing with too much force, you'll make good contact, which sends the ball running over the green. It's a ticklish situation.

There's only one way I know to control consistently your distance from Kikuyu rough: play the shot as though it were a bunker shot. Use the same principles we discussed in Chapter 4 for the basic bunker shot. Open your stance and your sand wedge the appropriate amount for the distance of this particular pitch or chip shot. Aim for the leading edge of your wedge to strike the grass about two inches behind the ball. Make the same slicing action with the right hand under and through the ball as from a good lie in a bunker.

The ball should come out high and soft, so that it won't run too far after landing. (Expect a little more release than you would from an actual bunker shot from the same distance.) Practice this technique and you'll quickly gain confidence in the shot and a feel for hitting the ball a particular distance.

Dig from a Divot

We've all experienced the frustration of hitting a nice drive in the fairway, only to find the ball lying in a divot hole. Still, to recover, you must stay cool and focused. If you don't have longer than middle-iron distance left to the green, there's no reason the shot can't be played successfully. Here's how to recover.

Move the ball back in your stance, with hands ahead, and keep most of your weight on your left side. Make a steeper-than-normal,

To recover from a divot, swing the club down hard into the ball while keeping a firm hold with your left hand.

three-quarter backswing for better balance and control. Swing the club back down hard into the ball while keeping a firm hold with your left hand.

The ball should come out in a low trajectory and roll more than normal as well. To compensate, take a more lofted club (say, a seven-iron instead of a six-iron) for the distance at hand.

Navigating the "Skip" Shot

Let's say you've found yourself behind tree branches that require you to hit a low shot, but you must get the ball across a water hazard that extends all the way to the green. Although it sounds like an impossible shot, it's not—if you know how to play the "skip" shot across the water.

First, visualize the shot you need to hit—a low, hard slice that will skip on the water twice before hopping out onto the green on the other side. Once you've visualized the flight, select the club you'll need to produce it—either a two-, three-, or four-iron.

Next, set up for a low slice by aligning the clubface square to the target, with your body aligned well left. The ball should be placed opposite the center of your stance. Use the swing you would for the wind cheater described earlier. Swing around a steady head and spine.

The low slicing action you impart to the ball will keep it skimming and give it a hard forward momentum that will help it skim across the water's surface. This is a "home run" shot that should only be used when you are factoring the all-or-none consequences of this play into your golf course situation.

The High Soft One

We've discussed several situations that call for you to give the ball a lower, more controlled trajectory. Now let's talk about when and how to hit the ball high.

A large percentage of the time, conditions on American courses favor high shots, especially because of their well-watered, manicured turf and tightly bunkered greens. The ability to land the ball

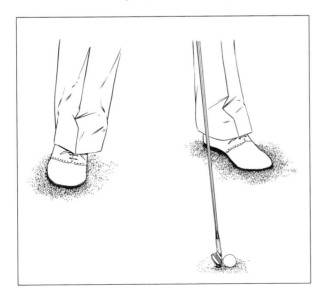

When setting up to play an extrahigh shot, play the ball well forward in your stance.

on a fairly small target area and make it stop quickly is a major benefit to good scoring. So let me tell you how it's done.

In setting up, play the ball high up off your left instep, grip the club lightly, put slightly more weight on your right foot, and keep your head well behind the ball.

Start the club back from the ball very slowly, concentrating on making a full shoulder turn and setting the club softly at the top.

Strive for a slow, smooth transition into the downswing, turning the hips fully through the impact zone. Release the club freely through the ball rather than hitting at it. The goal is to hit the ball on the upswing so that a little loft is added to the clubface. Focus on the loose recocking of the clubhead—up and to the left. Continue on into a full, balanced follow-through.

Any time you're playing downwind off the tee, the high soft one will get airborne quickly and provide a big distance boost. Into the greens, you can add even a little more stopping power by adjusting your stance just a touch open to put a trace of fade spin on the shot.

Last, when playing the high soft one from the fairway, remember to do so only when the lie is reasonably good.

Bank on It

A green-side spot you'll inevitably find from time to time is down a steep bank over the green. To compound the problem, the pin is on the back of a two-tiered green, so you can't stop the ball anywhere near the flag with a lofted pitch.

In this case, your smart play is to bank a running shot into the slope, so that it has enough momentum to bounce over the top, but not enough so that it runs well past the hole or off the green.

The technique here is not tricky. Play the shot like a firm-wristed chip, with your weight favoring your left side and the ball about centered in your stance. Concentrate on contacting the ball first and the turf second.

The key is to pick the club with the right loft for the particular situation. If the bank is very steep and the grass is long, you'll need to carry the ball higher up the bank to make sure it gets over the top. (*Note:* this is a tough bank shot, because it opens up the possibility of taking too much loft, making you carry the entire bank on the fly.) Chances are you'll be looking at using an eight- or nine-iron or, possibly, a pitching wedge in this scenario.

If the bank is not quite so steep or the grass is thinner, land the ball lower on the bank with a straighter-faced club, so that it runs up on the green. A five-, six-, or seven-iron will be your most likely choice here.

The tendency on the bank shot is to hit the ball too hard, so if anything, you get the ball over the bank all right, but it runs well past the hole. There's no substitute for practicing this specialty shot to learn the feel of the amount of bounce and roll you'll achieve.

The Green-side Pop

One of my favorite recovery shots is the short, lofted lob from a grassy green-side upslope.

If your lie is reasonably good, the shot is not difficult. Select your pitching wedge, sand wedge, or *L*-wedge, depending on how close

To hit the pop, concentrate on pointing the clubface toward the sky through impact.

the pin is to the edge of the green nearest you. Remember that since the ball is on an upslope, some extra loft will be added to the club-face so you'll hit the shot higher, softer, and shorter than normal.

At address, put a shade more weight than usual on your right, or lower, foot to help you maintain your balance and position your body perpendicular to the slope. Keep the clubface square to the hole. Make a slow, leisurely backswing, with a slight shoulder turn, and let your wrists hinge a bit at the top of the stroke.

Allow your wrists to uncock freely at the start of the downswing. Concentrate on keeping the clubface facing the sky through impact. Try to swing up the slope and make a firm hit.

Plan for the ball to carry most of the way to the hole, because it will drop onto the green at a steep angle.

Fairway Metal Bunker Play

Amateurs, more often than the pros, find themselves in a fairway bunker from which they can't get home with an iron club. If the circumstances are right, there's no reason you can't go for the green from this position with a fairway metal. Here are the "green light" criteria: (1) the lie must be good and (2) there must be almost no lip in front of you. Assuming you can go, here's how to proceed.

- I think the best play from here is a fade. So set the clubface at the target and align your body to the left. Hold the club slightly above the sand and visualize your clubhead path as shallow and along the sand.
- Choke down one-half inch on the grip.
- Position the ball opposite your left heel.
- Once you're set, concentrate on a very slow, wide take-away dominated by your arms; the downswing is similarly con-trolled by the arms, so that you sweep the club squarely into the back of the ball.

Using this technique, you'll find you can hit a fairway metal nearly as far as you can from a normal fairway lie—even all the way to the green.

The Lob from Rough to a Tight Pin

When you've missed the green and are in the rough without much green to work with, you need to take a bit more risk to get the ball close. Here you need to play a shot that's similar to the action of a short sand shot.

The key is how your ball is lying. If it's not all the way down in the rough, you have a big advantage, since you can open the clubface of your wedge somewhat and still get the leading edge under the ball.

This is a situation that's perfect for the *L*-wedge. It not only has more loft than the sand wedge but has a flange with less bounce, so it's safe to play out of grass.

Your setup and swing should be the same as for the short sand shot. Open the clubface and your stance goes left. Play the ball opposite your left heel to instep. Aim for the leading edge of the clubface to enter the rough two inches behind the ball. Make the same length swing you'd need for a sand shot of the same distance.

To play a lob shot from the rough to a pin placed close to the green's edge nearest you, set up with your stance and the clubface open.

Then go ahead and hit with a glancing blow.

The result should be an extrahigh soft shot, with little spin, that rolls only a few feet after it lands. Given a reasonable lie, I don't think there's any pin you can't get to with this shot, provided you have enough confidence to aggressively swipe under the ball and through the grass. Again, the more you develop your feel for the shot through practice, the closer to the hole you'll stop the ball in actual play.

Be Two Golfers in One

You'll run into situations in which your ball has come to rest near a tree and you can't get at it with a right-handed swing. This often occurs when the ball is just beyond a tree trunk.

Many of you who have watched me practice and warm up know that on occasion I will pretend I'm Phil Mickelson and swing the opposite way. The reason is that a number of years ago I was given the advice to employ a few of these swings each day to stretch the muscles on the right side of the back and shoulders because they are continually compressed in a very similar manner during the untold number of shots that any professional hits in the course of a career. It feels good to me and it makes sense. With my admitted joy in practicing varied shots, I have sometimes hit a few shots left-handed with the club turned upside-down on, say, a five-iron through wedge. I haven't used it very often in a tournament, but it's worked a number of times for me. My advice to you is to practice this technique over and over before you attempt to use it on the course. I'm no doctor, but it might just help keep your back healthy as well.

The Pitch to a Blind Green

On hilly courses you'll often encounter pitch shots in which all of the green and all or part of the flagstick are obscured from view. This adds greatly to the challenge of getting the ball close. You need to use good visualization skills in addition to making a sound execution of the stroke. Here's what to do.

1. If the shot is totally blind, walk up until you can see the entire flag and green. You want to know not only where the flag is but where you need to land the ball to get it close.

2. Step off the yardage as you walk to the green. When you reach the spot where you have a clear view (say it's forty yards from your ball), estimate the distance from there to the hole. Say it's another thirty-five yards. Now you know you have a pitch shot of seventy-five yards total, and having seen the land in front of the hole, you can estimate exactly how far the ball must carry.

3. Once you're back over the ball, pick the club and visualize the swing you'll need to execute the seventy-five-yard pitch. An extra practice swing or two may help.

4. Keep in mind that if the shot is uphill, you'll need a little more swing force to carry the distance. Concentrating on making a full finish will encourage that stronger swing.

Rough Recoveries

When you've driven the ball into rough, it's important that you develop a clear picture of how you want to execute your next shot. Basically, there are two ways to go in escaping rough on full shots. Which one to choose depends on a combination of factors: the depth (and moisture) of the grass, how deep the ball is sitting, the length of the shot remaining, whether you have a clear line to run the ball onto the green, whether you must carry the ball onto the green, and, finally, your own personal strength and ability to execute this style of shot.

On blind uphill pitch shots, concentrate on making a full finish to encourage a stronger swing.

The Punch Method

The punch method is the safer way to play from rough, and the one you should choose when the grass is deep or wet and the lie is poor. If the distance to the green isn't too far and you can run the ball on, you still may be able to reach the green. Or you might use this shot to produce as much yardage as you can and set yourself up for a pitch-and-putt par.

Your swing objective here is to hit down on the ball as sharply as you can to keep as little heavy grass as possible from getting between club and ball and muffling the shot. To accomplish this, position the ball at the center of or slightly behind the center of your stance, with your hands ahead of the clubface at address to promote a steep backswing arc. The clubface should remain square to slightly shut. Grip the club more firmly than normal with your left hand and place 60 to 70 percent of your weight on your left foot.

The swing should be dominated by the arms. Push the club straight back from the ball in an upright arc and reach your hands high. Then pull the club straight down into the back of the ball

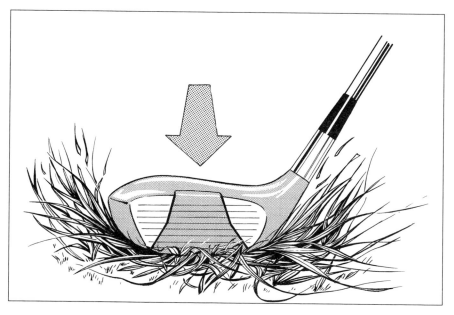

A lofted metal wood will usually work better than a long iron for a recovery from rough.

while keeping your head steady. Because the downswing is steep, your follow-through will be restricted.

The ball will come out lower than normal, with extra run. While it's very difficult to play this shot effectively with the low-lofted irons, you'll find a metal wood can come in very handy here. This is because the larger sole flattens out the grass behind the ball, so you get less resistance than you would with an iron, especially if you carry a utility wood in your bag, i.e., a six- or seven-wood.

The Rough Sweep

The rough sweep is the shot to hit if the rough is fairly light or the ball is sitting up fairly well. In these instances, some grass will still get between club and ball, causing it to fly farther than normal. To keep the ball under control, your best bet is to play a high shot with less club.

Address the ball a little forward of your normal position. Your weight should be slightly favoring your right foot to encourage a more sweeping motion. Set your clubface square to the target while aligning your body (and your grip) about ten yards left of your target. Make a slow, controlled backswing, with a nice full shoulder rotation. On the downswing, make the loose drop of your arms that creates a nice shallow clubhead path. Get the club through the grass and up on your left shoulder swiftly.

Proper impact will result in a high-flying shot that will curve slightly from left to right. Be prepared for the flyer effect that will make the ball go farther than on a clean lie. Those of you who generate relatively high clubhead speed will have the best result with this shot. My rule of thumb is that if the grass is light the ball will tend to fly right. If the grass is deep, the ball will tend to fly left.

The Hard Line on Hardpan

In setting up to play a shot on hardpan, position the ball back in your stance with your hands ahead of it. Grip the club firmly to prevent the clubface from opening at impact.

Make a fairly upright backswing. Pull the club down and through sharply, using a punching action. A crisp impact should produce a low, rising trajectory, along with good bite on the ball.

An important point to remember is that, depending on your own physical strength, you can only play the punch from hardpan down to a certain length of iron. Most golfers will find it difficult to get the ball airborne using this action off hardpan with longer than a four- or five-iron. What if the shot calls for a long iron or fairway wood?

In these cases, you can opt to hit the sweep from hardpan, clipping the ball cleanly up from the hard ground. To accomplish this, do the following.

1. Set up squarely to your target or a fraction open.
2. Play the ball directly opposite your left heel, so your hands are pretty much even with the ball.
3. Keep your weight evenly distributed at address.
4. Swing the club as you would from a nice normal lie, with your single swing thought being to revolve around a rock-steady spine angle; to ensure that you stay steady, swing at a slightly slower speed than normal.

To hit a punch shot off hardpan, play the ball back in your stance. This will encourage a steep backswing and sharp downswing.

COUPLES'S CLINIC

51 LIE DETECTION

Here's a tip most amateurs aren't aware of that's useful whenever you're facing an approach shot from medium to deep rough. You should judge not only how deep the ball is sitting in the grass but also whether the rough is lying with or against you.

If the rough is lying against you, that is, away from the hole, it will resist your clubhead more strongly than if it were standing straight. So you have to give this lie even more respect than usual when you're choosing a club. If the depth of rough is such that you'd normally figure a six-iron as the most club you could use, then play it safe and go to a seven- or eight-iron instead, so as to be sure to get the ball up and out of the grass.

If the grass is lying toward the hole, the rough's resistance is lessened and you can reasonably expect to hit a five- or four-iron when a six might be the maximum if the grass were straight up.

A couple of other points: One, when the rough is with you, you'll probably get a bit of flier effect. The total carry and roll will be at least one club longer than you'd normally get, whatever club you choose. Two, when the rough is against you, grip the club firmly and opt for the punch over the sweep.

52 LOOK, SEE

When you've jailed yourself in the woods, the standard advice is simply to punch the ball back to the fairway and go on from there. That's fine—if you truly have no other option. But I've seen a lot of amateurs fail to spot an opportunity to play from tree trouble all the way to the green or at least get very close to it.

When you hit a ball in the woods, think creatively. Can you hit a low shot under the trees and run the ball onto the green? Is there an opening in the branches that "fits" the trajectory you'd be likely to attain with the club that could get you all the way home? Do you have a springy lie that will allow you to fly the ball over all the trees? How about a hook or a slice around the obstacles? Which are you more proficient at, and will the lay of the land and the wind help either type of shot?

Finally, remember that there's nothing in the rules of golf that says you have to play out to your own fairway. If you can gain substantial yardage and an opening for your next shot by playing to another fairway, why not go for it? That's exactly what Ed Furgol did on the par-five seventy-second hole of the 1954 U.S. Open at Baltusrol in New Jersey. From the left woods, Furgol played his recovery onto a fairway of Baltusrol's adjacent Upper Course. It paid off—Furgol parred and won the open.

Creative "seeing" like this will save you strokes and matches too.

53 BREATHE EASY

Before you step up to any shot from deep trouble, especially in a tight match, make it a point to take a couple of deep breaths. There is a tendency to get more anxious than normal when playing from tough course situations that you're not used to. Ironically, this is when you need to stay especially cool. A couple of deep breaths will help you focus intently on the basic execution of the shot at hand, rather than getting you on a negative track about what might happen next or about being in trouble in the first place and hurriedly hitting a poorly executed shot.

54 PLAY HARDBALL

Under most conditions I (as do most PGA Tour pros) play a relatively soft balata-covered golf ball. This ball allows you a greater amount of backspin as well as a better ability to curve the ball in either direction.

However, when the wind starts gusting, a balata ball presents more of a problem. In heavy winds, you generally don't want a lot of backspin on the ball, which makes it fly higher and thus become more susceptible to heavy gusts. So even some Tour players find it an advantage to play a harder, surlyn-covered ball in heavy wind. The surlyn ball will take on a lower backspin rate so it tends to bore through the wind more readily. Manufacturers have made great strides in golf ball technology and there are numerous combinations of dimple designs and substances used in construction. In this particular case, you're looking for a two-piece surlyn-covered ball with a low spin rate.

I suggest that you take advantage and play a hard ball when the winds are up. Furthermore, if you have persistent problems with a severe hook or slice, keep in mind that the harder ball will also slightly reduce those flight patterns in normal conditions, although the long-term solution of working on your game is still advised.

55 IN THE GROOVE

I often play golf with amateurs, the majority of whom don't keep the faces of their irons clean. This is an unfortunate oversight. When you let dirt and grass build up in the grooves of your irons, the clubface can't grip the ball and put backspin on it. The result: an uncontrollable shot that usually flies over the green into trouble.

No Tour player would allow this to happen, and neither

should you. Every couple of rounds at least, rinse off your club-faces in warm, soapy water, and clean out the grooves with a sharp golf tee, brush, or pocketknife. Give yourself use of all the control that was built into the club.

56 GRIP TIP

As with the clubfaces, you also owe it to yourself to keep the grip end of each of your clubs clean and tacky. You just won't believe how many amateur golfers play with badly worn-out grips. They're putting themselves at an unbelievable disadvantage.

You see, when someone grips a golf club, he or she will instinctively grip it and hold it throughout the swing with the amount of tension needed to keep the club from slipping in any way. The more worn the grips are, the tighter the golfer must grip throughout the swinging action. This most often leads to an overall tensing of the hands and arms that, in turn, results in a big loss in both swing freedom and clubhead speed. I'm willing to bet that if your grips are currently in very poor shape, you'll hit the ball ten yards farther and a lot straighter just by putting a fresh set of properly fitting grips on your clubs. It's a small investment that's well worth it.

57 GIVE YOUR SWING A HAND

If you're like most amateur golfers, you probably wonder how the pros hit the ball so far. Well, I'll tell you, it's got little to do with strength. The pros aren't necessarily much stronger (if at all) than many amateurs. However, they use what they have much more effectively. A professional uses a coordinated effort of the hands, arms, and body to create a really free swing of the clubhead. On the other hand, most amateurs, either by trying to control the ball or hit it hard, overuse the upper body and have a tense-looking action that seldom produces the desired outcome. Here's a couple of simple practice drills to improve your swinging action.

Address the ball with only your right hand on the club (and your left hand behind your back). Make a nice shoulder turn and swing the club back and through with a loose hinging of your right wrist and elbow. Now try the same thing with your left hand only (and your right hand behind your back). Again, feel the shoulders turn and your left arm and elbow cock and hinge. At first, you may not be able to control the club. Gradually, though, you'll build up both strength and coordination of motion, with the end result being an improved swing.

Practice hitting only one-handed shots with short to medium irons. After about twenty shots, put both hands on the club and swing. You feel like Freddie Couples, right?

58 UP AGAINST THE WALL

You may have noticed that I have a fairly upright arm swing, even though I'm not exceptionally tall (five feet, eleven inches). I see far more high handicappers whose swings are too flat (meaning too much like a baseball swing, or too horizontal) than I do amateurs who are too upright. The results are usually low, powerless shots that either hook or nosedive into the ground.

Here's a good way to check your swing plane and correct it if necessary. Take an old driver and assume your normal address position while standing with your heels three feet away from a wall. Next, swing the club up to the top in slow-motion fashion. Did that clubhead hit the wall? If it did, your swing is probably too flat. Practice turning your shoulders to the top, while you watch the club, and keep the arms swinging and cocking up so that the clubhead never quite touches the wall.

After reworking your plane, you'll find you'll get a lot more height and accuracy on your shots. *One last piece of advice to aid relations at home:* select a wall that's not too big a problem to hit with a club—for example, a garage wall might fare better than one in your living room.

59 BALANCING ACT

Good balance is absolutely essential in any golf swing. Unfortunately, most of us get so carried away searching for distance that we might forget this simple truism. The result: missed shots and lost distance.

To improve your balance and control, work this technique into your practice sessions: try hitting short irons off a tee, say a seven-iron, with a controlled, balanced swing, while keeping your *eyes closed.* The first few times you try it, you'll probably feel as if you're going to whiff. Stay with this "shut-eye" swing for a while. Gradually, your contact will improve as you learn to sustain good balance throughout the swing. Once you get a good feel with your eyes closed, try to maintain this identical swing feel in actual play. If you can accomplish this, you'll probably shoot your best score of the year.

60 COUNT YOUR BLESSINGS

When you've hit a poor shot and find yourself in trouble, train yourself never to become truly upset. Maybe you've played ten or twelve holes very well to this point. There's no reason to let one bad shot ruin a good round.

Even if you aren't having an extra-good day, you should

always count your blessings. Be thankful that you are able to be out on a beautiful course playing. Many people in this world don't have that opportunity, for one reason or another.

When you think within this positive framework, the trouble you're in stops looking like the end of the world. Now you can go ahead and use some of the mental and physical techniques I've described to get yourself back in play.

ONE LAST TIP

I've enjoyed sharing with you the many tips and information in this book. I hope that reading *Total Shotmaking* will help you have fun and improve at the sport we both love so much. As you can tell, I'm a big advocate of taking a few good ideas and working them slowly into your game. As you do so, don't hesitate to seek out your favorite teaching professional. He or she can really save you time in the learning process. Good luck! See you on the course. Just like you, I'm still becoming the total shotmaker.

ABOUT THE AUTHOR

John Andrisani is the senior editor of instruction at *GOLF Magazine* and a former assistant editor of Britain's *Golf Illustrated* magazine.

Andrisani has coauthored major instruction books with the game's top Tour pros: *Learning Golf: The Lyle Way,* with Sandy Lyle; *Natural Golf,* with Seve Ballesteros; and *101 Supershots,* with Chi Chi Rodriguez. He is also the coauthor of *The Golf Doctor* with Robin McMillan; *Hit It Hard!* with power hitter Mike Dunaway; *Golf Your Way: An Encyclopedia of Instruction,* with teacher Phil Ritson; and *Grip It and Rip It!* with John Daly.

Andrisani's popular instructional articles and humorous golf stories have appeared in golfing and nongolfing publications worldwide, including *GOLF France* and *Playboy.*

A former holder of the American Golf Writer's Championship, Andrisani plays off a four handicap at Lake Nona Golf Club in Orlando, Florida.

Andrisani was recently selected to appear in *Who's Who in America.*